P9-DCX-641

MANAGING IN TURBULENT TIMES

Books by Peter F. Drucker

Managing in Turbulent Times

Adventures of a Bystander

The Unseen Revolution

Management: Tasks, Responsibilities, Practices

Men, Ideas, and Politics

Technology, Management, and Society

The Age of Discontinuity

The Effective Executive

Managing for Results

Landmarks of Tomorrow

America's Next Twenty Years

The Practice of Management

The New Society

Concept of the Corporation

The Future of Industrial Man

The End of Economic Man

MANAGING IN TURBULENT TIMES

by Peter F. Drucker

This is a special edition prepared for
The Presidents Association.

HARPER & ROW, PUBLISHERS

NEW YORK

Cambridge
Hagerstown
Philadelphia
San Francisco

1817

London
Mexico City
São Paulo
Sydney

FIRST EDITION

Designer: Sidney Feinberg

Library of Congress Cataloging in Publication Data

Drucker, Peter Ferdinand, 1909–
  Managing in turbulent times.

  Includes index.
  1. Industrial management.   I. Title.
HD31.D7734   658   79-3389
ISBN 0-06-011094-5

---

80 81 82 83 84 10 9 8 7 6 5 4 3 2 1

Contents

MANAGING   IN   TURBULENT   TIMES

Introduction

Last June, I spoke in London at a meeting of British managers; the topic was "Can Managers Manage?" Many of the discussants seemed to think that the answer is a clear "No." But, of course, the question is meaningless. Managers have no choice but to try. Managing effectively is what they are being paid for, managing effectively is the only reason for the existence of managers and management.

There are undoubtedly a great many—indeed, far too many—things that managers, whether of business or of non-business public service institutions, *cannot* do, are not allowed to do, are impeded in doing. But this book focuses on actions, strategies, opportunities. It focuses on what managers *can* do, *should* do, *must* do.

Or rather it focuses on action, strategies, opportunities in the reverse order: *"must"* comes first, then *"should,"* and then *"can."* For the one certainty about the times ahead, the times in which managers will have to work and to perform, is that they will be turbulent times. And in turbulent times, the first task of management is to make sure of the institution's capacity for survival, to make sure of its structural strength and soundness, of its capacity to survive a blow, to adapt to sudden change, and to avail itself of new opportunities.

This book thus starts out with managing the fundamentals—inflation and liquidity, productivities and the costs of staying in business that are so misleadingly called "profit."

But managing the fundamentals also means managing for tomorrow. It means sloughing off yesterday, managing growth with a growth policy, growth strategies, and a way to distinguish between healthy growth, putting on fat, or cancer. It means knowing what strategies are available and how to choose among them. It requires the ability today to judge managerial performance in the areas that shape a business's tomorrow.

These, it may be said, are obvious—fundamentals always are. But how many managements work on them; how many even think of them?

Turbulence, by definition, is irregular, non-linear, erratic. But its underlying causes can be analyzed, predicted, managed. What management should—and can—manage is the single most important new reality underlying a great deal of the turbulence around: the sea-change in population structure and population dynamics, and especially the shifts in population structure and population dynamics in the developed countries of the West and Japan. These shifts are already changing the modes of economic integration throughout the world. They are likely to lead to a new "transnational confederation" based on production sharing and market control, replacing in many areas the old "multinational corporation" based on financial control. They are creating new consumer markets and realigning existing old consumer markets. They drastically change the labor force to the point where there will only be "labor forces," each with different expectations and different characteristics. They will force us to abandon altogether the concept of a "fixed retirement age." And they create a new demand on management—as well as a new opportunity—to make organized plans for redundancy.

Finally, there are new realities, new opportunities, and new threats in the environments of enterprise and institution: in the world economy and its integration side by side with increasing fragmentation of the world polity; in the emergence of the "employe society" in all developed non-Communist countries; in the metamorphosis of political order and political process.

Some time during the 1970s, the longest period of continuity in economic history came to an end. At some time during the last ten years we moved into turbulence.

The twenty-five years from the Marshall Plan to the mid-seventies were not only a period of unprecedented economic growth, the period of fastest and broadest growth the world economy has ever seen. They were also a period of high predictability. Socially, these were years of rapid changes. But economically, growth in the major countries proceeded in these years along lines that had been laid out before World War II, and in most cases well before the Great Depression. And the new growth during these years, the very rapid growth of a number of "secondary" countries—Brazil, for instance, Mexico, South Korea, or the non-Communist Chinese territories of Hong Kong, Taiwan, and Singapore—also proceeded along traditional and well-understood lines. From now on, growth is likely to be anything but "traditional"—and there is likely to be a good deal of it, even in the event of a severe depression.

These twenty-five years were also a period of high technological continuity, despite all the talk of the rapid pace of technological change. While there was rapid change indeed, it was mostly in areas that were already well mapped before World War II, in areas based on discoveries and innovations that had been made before the Great Depression and, in many cases, before World War I. This has ended. In technology, too, we are entering a period of turbulence, a period of rapid innovation, a period of fast and radical structural shifts.

In the twenty-five years after World War II, planning became fashionable. But planning, as commonly practiced, assumes a high degree of continuity. Planning starts out, as a rule, with the trends of yesterday and projects them into the future—using a different "mix" perhaps, but with very much the same elements and the same configuration. This is no longer going to work. The most probable assumption in a period of turbulence is the unique event which changes the configuration—and unique events cannot, by definition, be "planned." But they can often be foreseen. This requires strategies for tomorrow, strategies that anticipate where the greatest changes are likely to occur and what they are likely to be, strategies that enable a business—or a hospital, a school, a university—to take advantage of new realities and to convert turbulence into opportunity.

This book deals with the strategies needed to use rapid changes as opportunities, the strategies needed to convert the threat of change into opportunities for productive and profitable action, and for contribution alike to society, economy, and individual.

A time of turbulence is a dangerous time, but its greatest danger is a temptation to deny reality. The new realities fit neither the assumptions of the Left nor those of the Right. They do not mesh at all with "what everybody knows." They differ even more from what everybody, regardless of political persuasion, still believes reality to be. "What is" differs totally from what both Right and Left believe "ought to be." The greatest and most dangerous turbulence today results from the collision between the delusions of the decisionmakers, whether in governments, in the top managements of businesses, or in union leadership, and the realities.

But a time of turbulence is also one of great opportunity for those who can understand, accept, and exploit the new realities. It is above all a time of opportunity for leadership. One constant theme of this book is therefore the need for the decisionmaker in the individual enterprise to face up to reality and to resist the temptation of what "everybody knows," the temptation of the certainties of yesterday, which are about to become the deleterious superstitions of tomorrow.

This book discusses the new realities. But it is concerned with action rather than with understanding, with decisions rather than with analysis. It is not a "philosophical" book, nor does it ask: "Where are we going?" It aims at being practical, a work for the decisionmaker in whatever field of management, public or private. It is not a "how to" book. Rather, it tries to tell executives what to do.

PETER F. DRUCKER

Claremont, California
New Year's Day, 1980

1

Managing the Fundamentals

Managing the Fundamentals

In turbulent times, an enterprise has to be managed *both* to withstand sudden blows and to avail itself of sudden unexpected opportunities. This means that in turbulent times the fundamentals have to be managed, and managed well.

In predictable times, such as we lived through in the twenty-five years between the Marshall Plan and the OPEC cartel, the fundamentals tend to be taken for granted. But the fundamentals deteriorate unless they are being managed carefully, consistently, conscientiously, and all the time. Indeed, the greatest danger to most enterprises today—businesses, non-businesses, and public service institutions alike—may not be public hostility to business, environmental constraints, over-zealous regulations, energy, or even inflation. It may be a hidden deterioration in the fundamentals. After a long period of relative tranquillity there is always the danger of unexpected and hidden weak spots in the areas everybody takes for granted, everybody considers boring routine.

Fundamentals do not change. But the specifics to manage them do change greatly with changes in internal and external conditions. Managing in turbulent times thus has to begin with a discussion of the new and different demands affecting the fundamentals of survival and success in the existing business. These are:

—liquidity,
—productivities, and
—the costs of the future.

To manage the present business is not enough; but it has to come first.

Adjusting for Inflation

Before one can manage successfully, it is necessary to know precisely what one is managing. But executives today—both in businesses and in non-business public service institutions—do not know the facts. What they think are facts are largely illusions and half-truths. The reality of their enterprise is hidden, distorted and deformed by inflation. Executives today have available to them many times the reports, information, and figures their predecessors had; they have become dependent on these figures and are thus endangered if the figures lie to them. During inflation, however, the figures lie. Money still tends to be considered the standard of value and to be a value in itself, but in inflation this is a delusion. Before the fundamentals can be managed, the facts about any business—its sales, its financial position, its assets and liabilities, and its earnings—must be adjusted for inflation.

In the Western countries and in Japan, business after business these last ten years has announced "record profits" year after year. In fact, very few businesses (if any) in these countries can have made a profit at all. Making a profit is by definition impossible in an inflationary period, because inflation is the systematic destruction of wealth by government. The public, it should be said, senses this even though it does not understand it. This explains why the announcement of these "record profits" is being greeted with such skepticism by the stock exchange and with hostility by the public at large. But the illusion of "record profits" also leads to the wrong actions, the wrong decisions, the wrong analysis of the business. It leads to gross mismanagement.

All this is known to most executives. Yet few so far have even tried to correct the misinformation inflation creates. We know what to do and it is not very difficult. We need to adjust sales, prices, inventory, receivables, fixed assets and their depreciation, and earnings to inflation—not with total precision but within a reasonable range of probability. Until this is done, even the most knowledgeable executive will remain the victim of the illusions inflation creates. He may know that the figures he gets are grossly misleading; but as long as these are the figures he has in front of him, he will act on them rather than on his own better knowledge. And he will act foolishly, wrongly, irresponsibly.

A second dangerous deception is the belief that "earnings" shown because the enterprise still has the use of money obtained when costs of capital were lower (such as long-term debentures issued in pre-inflationary times and at pre-inflationary interest rates) are the true earnings of a business. Sooner or later (usually sooner) the money has to be replaced; and then the earnings must be adequate to cover the costs of capital at the time of refinancing. In adjusting for inflation, money in the business has to be adjusted just the same way as any other fixed asset—and it is an axiom that interest rates will always equal the rate of inflation.

"Inventory profits" are never real profits. If inflation continues, the inventory will have to be replaced at tomorrow's higher prices. If inflation stops, inventory profits immediately turn into an inventory loss. In either case, the apparent "inventory profit" is more properly a contingency reserve.

One reason why executives in most countries and the great majority of companies do not adjust to inflation is the belief that inflation is a "transitory phenomenon." But this, after fifteen years of unremitting inflation, can hardly be considered rational. Another reason is that governments, with rare exceptions—Brazil is the most important one—resist the truth about inflation. Governments, especially under the twentieth-century system of progressive income taxes, are the main beneficiaries of inflation and have no incentive at all to reveal the true facts. In some countries, notably the United States, the tax system has given executives a powerful incentive for lying to themselves. The U.S. tax system greatly favors stock options and bonuses tied to reported earnings, making it very much to the executives' self-interest to report inflated earnings. But in countries where stock options or bonuses of this kind are unknown, such as Japan, executives resist just as strenuously attempts at any adjustment of their reported figures to inflation. The major reason is surely vanity: executives like to take credit for "record earnings" even when they know that the figures are mere delusion, and indeed dishonesty.

One often hears the argument, especially from accountants, that figures should not be adjusted since there is no accurate method known for doing so. But this is very much as if physicians unable to agree on the precise treatment for a very sick patient were to declare him totally fit, his raging fever mere illusion. In any case, most of the figures that accountants work out down to the last penny are, as every accountant knows, estimates within a fairly wide range of probability, such as the range of error plus or minus 20 percent that applies to the balance-sheet figure for fixed assets.

Not to adjust to inflation is slothful and irresponsible. Managing in turbulent times must begin with the adjustment of the enterprise's figures to inflation, roughly yet within a realistic range of probabilities. The executive who fails to do so tries to deceive others. He only deceives himself.

Managing for Liquidity and Financial Strength

A constant complaint during the last few years has been that "Stock market prices are much too low." Companies, it is pointed out again and again, sell at ludicrously low price/earnings ratios and often well below their reported book value or their liquidating value. But these complaints are groundless, by and large. It can even be argued that stock market prices are far too high, considering the uncertainties not only of the future but of the present. If companies' accounts were adjusted for inflation, the earnings of many would turn into losses. What look like very low price/earnings ratios might then turn out to be high ratios between earnings in constant currency values and stock market prices. And if companies' balance sheets were adjusted for inflation, the book values of many companies, and certainly those of most manufacturing companies, would be significantly lower and might even show an excess of liabilities over assets.

Above all, the stock market increasingly values companies according to their liquidity rather than by their earnings. The quotations on every major stock exchange—New York and London, Zurich, Tokyo, and Frankfurt—correlate quite closely with cash flow and liquidity, and very poorly, if at all, with the inflation-distorted earnings figures. The stock markets are right. In turbulent times, liquidity is more important than earnings. A business—but equally a public service institution—can survive long periods of low earnings or low revenues if it has adequate cash flow and financial strength. The opposite is not true. It is rational of the stock market to price companies by their financial position rather than by their earnings. And liquidity, unlike reported earnings, is a reasonably reliable measure even in inflationary times.

In turbulent times, the balance sheet becomes more important than the profit and loss statement. In turbulent times, in other words, management has to put financial strength before earnings. In turbulent times, it is essential to know the minimum liquidity needed to stay in business. What working capital does *our* business need to survive a ninety-day or hundred-and-twenty-day panic? After a hundred and twenty days of panic there is always a new "normality." But during the panic a business has to be able to stay afloat without outside help or it risks foundering. It has to have the liquid resources needed to keep going, if only on an austerity basis. In turbulent times, businesses need to think through what they could and would do, should they be forced to survive a panic, a credit crunch, or a sudden deflationary downturn. Concern for sales and market position, innovation and earnings, has to be balanced in such times with concern for financial strength, solvency, and liquidity. Liquidity by itself is not an objective. But in turbulent times it becomes a restraint. It becomes a survival need.

Managing Productivities

Making resources productive is the specific job of management, as distinct from the other jobs of the "manager": entrepreneurship and administration. The history of management as a distinct social function began a hundred years ago with the discovery that resources can be managed for productivity. It is only managers—not nature or laws of economics or governments—that make resources productive. Resources can be made productive in the individual plant or enterprise, the individual store, the individual hospital, the individual office, the individual port, the individual research laboratory. They are made productive—or deprived of productivity—by individual managers within their own individual sphere of responsibility.

A century ago, Karl Marx in the last, unfinished volume of *Das Kapital* based his most confident prediction of the "imminent demise" of what we now call "capitalism" (a term coined only after Marx's death) on the "inexorable law of the diminishing productivity of capital." Marx was repeating what every nineteenth-century economist before him had accepted as axiomatic. And if there is really such a "law" of the declining productivity of "capital" (or of any other resource), every economic system would indeed be doomed.

But by one of those ironies of which the muse of history is so fond, the continuous and purposeful increase of productivity through management was discovered just about when Marx so confidently predicted its "inexorable decline." This discovery also explains why not one of the other "certainties" that were "scientific truths" for Karl Marx—the pauperization of the working class, the concentration of wealth in the hands of fewer and fewer "exploiters," or the polarization of society between a very small and shrinking group of "owners" and a large, growing mass of proletarian "wage slaves"—has occurred in developed countries, countries that have developed managers and management.

The turning point was Frederick W. Taylor's discovery, around 1875, that work could be managed and thereby made more productive. Before Taylor, the only way to get more output was to work harder and longer. But Taylor saw that the way to get more output was to "work smarter," that is, more productively. He saw that the productivity of work is not the responsibility of the worker but of the manager. Taylor also saw—although he never formulated the insight into a theory—that productivity is the result of the application to work of the specific human capital resource, knowledge.

Taylor applied knowledge to human labor and, in accordance with the nineteenth-century realities, to manual labor.

We now know that knowledge has to be applied to all resources: capital, key physical resources, time, and knowledge itself. Indeed, we now know that a valid theory of economics will have to be based on productivity as the source of value. The nineteenth-century labor theory of value, which Marx took unchanged from his predecessors all the way back to Ricardo and Adam Smith, was simply wrong; even the Marxists have had to give it up. But the valiant attempt to do without a theory of value altogether—begun a hundred years ago by the Austrian school and climaxing in the "value-free" economic analysis of today's Keynesians and Friedmanites— has also been proved a failure. We do need a genuine economic theory based on a theory of value; but such a theory will have to be based on the postulate that "productivity is the source of all economic value."

By now we know quite a bit about increasing productivity. We know that it is in part achieved by innovation, the shift of resources from old and declining employments to new and more productive ones. In part, productivity is increased through the continuous improvement of the productivity of the resources in existing employments. We know that we need to work on the productivity of each of the factors of production: capital, natural resources, time, and knowledge. But we know also that what counts in the end is total overall productivity of *all* resources in a given process, a given enterprise, a given economic employment.

And above all we know that productivities are created and destroyed, improved or damaged, in what we call the "microeconomy": the individual enterprise, plant, shop, or office. Productivities are the responsibility of management.

For the last century productivities have been rising steadily in all developed countries, or at least in all countries with market economies. Wherever there has been economic development in a country, it has been based on the purposeful management of resources for increased productivity. This does not apply to manufacturing alone. Productivities have increased even faster in that sector in which, as every economist of the nineteenth century (including Marx) "knew," there could not be any productivity increase at all: agriculture. Indeed, nothing has changed the economic landscape quite so much between the nineteenth century and the twentieth as the explosion of productivity in the farms of the industrialized, developed countries. But the physician of today is also many times more productive than the physician of 1900. Doctors eighty years ago spent most of their time contemplating the rear end of a horse as they made their slow way from one outlying farmhouse to the next. The physician of 1980 lives in a metropolitan area where his patients are densely settled; and thanks to the automobile, even a sick child can be brought to his office in safety and comfort. Today's physician can see in the course of one working day about ten times as many patients as his predecessors did eighty years ago. And without technical innovation, simply by constant work on better management, the productivity of one dollar employed in the commercial bank is today about a hundred_times what it was a century ago—one dollar of deposits in a commercial bank now supports about a hundred times the volume of transactions it did in the late nineteenth century.

This explosive expansion of productivities has totally changed the way we look at economies and economics. Marx and the entire nineteenth century took for granted the "law of diminishing returns." Hence they focused on increasing supply, on microeconomics. By the end of the first quarter of this century, expanding productivities had made this concern appear unnecessary or at least old-fashioned. Productivities, it seemed, take care of themselves. So the economist's concern shifted to demand, and with it to macroeconomics. Keynes was perfectly aware of the total absence of any concern with productivity in his theory. When challenged on this point, as he frequently was in the early days of his Cambridge seminar, he would always answer that productivity would be taken care of by businessmen if given the right macroeconomics, that is, the right demand policies.

In the context of the 1920s during which Keynes developed his thoughts, this was a tenable position. It no longer is so today. After a century of steady increase in the productivity of all resources, productivities have become stagnant and have actually been going down in all major developed countries these last ten or fifteen years. The decline began in the 1960s well before OPEC. It began even before the rapid increase in the rate of inflation—in fact, the increase in the rate of inflation is in itself in large part a consequence of the slowdown in the increase in productivity. The slowdown in productivities also began before the developed countries imposed an ever-increasing burden of controls and regulations on the productive sectors of the economy. There is no doubt that the tremendous amount of new regulations, whether in regard to the environment, to safety, to employment practices, or whatever, has seriously impeded productivities. But it is by no means the only, and may not even be the major factor.

Productivities have become endangered because they have been neglected. It was not only Keynes who believed that productivities would take care of themselves; increasingly, managers have done so too. But nothing is as dangerous as a decrease in productivities. It makes a shrinking of the economy inevitable. It creates inflationary pressures, social conflict, and mutual suspicion. Marx was absolutely right in postulating that no system could survive a shrinking in the productivity of capital—or in the productivity of any key resource.

The sharp slowdown in productivity is not confined to the non-Communist countries. On the contrary, the decline—

especially in the productivity of capital—is in all likelihood far greater in the Soviet Union and in the developed countries of the Soviet system (Russia's European satellites) than it is in the non-Communist countries of the West or in Japan. But this is cold comfort. It does not help the dying cancer patient to know that the patient in the next bed is terminally ill.

To reverse the trend in productivities is thus a major managerial task. It is the single most important contribution managers of major institutions, whether business or public service institutions, could make toward calming the turbulence. At the same time, for their own institutions to survive, let alone to prosper, managers need to work continuously on improving productivities.

The productivity of all resources can be substantially improved in most institutions, and in relatively short order. "What one man has done, another man can always do again," says a very old proverb. In every economy, in every industry, and in every branch of human activity, there are institutions that operate at a substantially higher productivity level than the average. What makes one company stand out and lead in any one industry, in any one economy, in any one area, is that it operates at about twice the average productivity of its industry, its economy, or its area. Above all, the leading company always operates at about twice the average productivity of capital.

Marx was right: Capital comes first. Capital is the future.

In the United States the General Electric Company, for example, does not owe its leadership position primarily to technological achievement. What sets it apart from Westinghouse, its closest competitor and the industry's number two, is above all productivity of capital. GE gets about twice as much work out of a dollar as Westinghouse does. The same holds true for Siemens compared to the rest of the electrical apparatus industry of Europe. And in Great Britain, Sir

Arnold Weinstock succeeded within ten or fifteen years in converting a dying British General Electric Company into a leader by doubling the productivity of capital, without in any way "sweating labor" or "exploiting labor." Weinstock is able to pay his employees more and to give them steadier employment precisely because the productivity of capital is high in his company. In Great Britain too, one retail chain, Marks and Spencer, leads the pack primarily because it gets almost twice as much sales out of a unit of shelf space or a square foot of store area as other British or European retailers do. There is no secret to these higher productivities. There is only persistent, hard, steady work and a commitment to managing productivities.

This commitment is now required of all managers in developed countries. To fulfill it, they must set two goals in their institutions. The first is to double the productivity of money in the business—the productivity of capital—within the next eight to ten years, at an annual rate of productivity increase of about 7½ percent. The second is to aim at being able to produce at least 50 percent more within the next eight to ten years without increasing the number of people employed; this means that they must aim to raise the productivity of people at an annual rate of 4 to 5 percent. Both goals are attainable. Both require only hard work.

Four key resources have to be managed consistently, systematically, and conscientiously for productivity. They are capital, crucial physical assets, time, and knowledge. Each of these resources has to be managed separately and differently.

Most managers know approximately how many times a year their enterprise turns over the money invested in it. But, many managers think that it makes a difference whether the money is "our own" or "borrowed," whether it is "debt" or "equity." In fact, it makes absolutely no difference to the productivity of money who the legal owner is or what the legal terms are. Money is money—and all money, regardless of source or legal obligation, costs roughly the same. Furthermore, a manager has to know specifically where the money is invested in a particular enterprise—one cannot manage an aggregate. The first step toward managing the productivity of capital is to know where all the money in the business really is; then one can start managing the important employments of capital. In one business this may be receivables, that is, the credit extended by a business to its customers. A non-banking business—a manufacturer, for example—cannot compete with the banks in granting credit. He has to pay both the bank's costs of obtaining and administering money and his own. Hence he has to think through what he expects to get back when he extends a loan to a customer—something too few businesses have done. But the money may also be in fixed assets, in shelf space or selling space in the retail store, for instance, in which case what needs to be managed is turnover and revenues per shelf unit or shelf space over selling time. Or the money may be in expensive machinery—and nothing is quite as unproductive and wasteful of capital as idle time of expensive machinery. Yet the accounting model rarely provides that information; indeed, the assumptions of "standard costs" in the typical cost-accounting system conceal it. In the typical university the capital investment—an extremely expensive one—is in classrooms and laboratory buildings that are being used only a few hours a day, four or five days a week. By developing effective continuing-education programs for highly motivated adults in the late afternoon and evening hours and at weekends, a university may well double the productivity of its capital within a few short years, particularly if it is located in an urban environment. But the first and most important step always is to find out where the money is. The data are in the information base of the accounting model and can be obtained fairly easily, *if the executive only asks for them.*

All institutions are alike in respect to three of the four key resources—capital, time, and knowledge. These three are universal. But different institutions differ greatly in respect to the fourth resource: their crucial physical resources. An ingot of copper is the critical material for the manufacturer of copper wire. It would be meaningless for the hospital, where the "patient bed" might be the key unit. Each institution needs to think through what the appropriate key physical unit or asset for its business is. It should then be fairly easy to manage it. Hospitals, for instance, have been able to increase the productivity of their crucial assets a great deal by realizing that the term "hospital bed" is a meaningless one. There are many kinds of hospital beds. The hospital bed for the acutely sick patient is very different, for instance, from the hospital bed needed for maternity (not a disease), or from that for patients staying in the hospital for diagnosis, for recovery from surgery, or for the period until the cast on a recently operated ankle dries.

Most managers believe that it is obvious what the key physical resource of their business is. Yet, as the hospital example shows, defining a key physical resource is risky and may be a difficult decision. Key physical assets, like all resources, require productivity goals with deadlines and a feedback from results to expectations. Just how much can be achieved in this area has been shown by the few companies that worked seriously on the productivity of energy after OPEC first raised petroleum prices. Long before OPEC, Dow Chemical in the United States had the reputation of doing an outstanding job in energy conservation. Yet Dow went to work on managing the productivity of energy when OPEC raised petroleum prices. It then succeeded in cutting its energy requirements in half in the five years 1974 to 1979, without any increase in the use of any other resource. This represents an annual productivity increase in the use of energy of 8 to 10 percent.

The Productivity of the Knowledge Worker

To manage the productivity of people, and especially of those highly qualified people who are potentially most productive but also most expensive, managers need to know the tasks to which such workers are assigned. It is not enough to know that John Smith works in accounting. If John Smith performs—and otherwise he should not be in accounting at all—we have to know what he is specifically assigned to do. Productivity of the human resource, and especially of knowledge workers, requires that people are assigned where the potential for results are, and not where their skill and knowledge cannot produce results no matter how well they work. Assignment control is the key to the productivity of the skilled worker.

This requires, first, that we know the strengths of people, and particularly of those with a proven record of performance. What do they do well? Where do they belong? It requires, secondly, that as far as possible people are assigned where the application of their strengths can produce results. It requires that they are assigned to opportunities, and those opportunities that are the right ones for them. When Frederick W. Taylor set out a century ago to make manual work productive, he assumed that there would be "one right way" to do specific manual operations, which would fit the great majority of people engaged in this work. He assumed that most people are "average." But his assumption has proved wrong, especially for work requiring skill and knowledge. When we talk of work that requires more than routine performance, obeying orders, doing repetitive unskilled motions, we have to assume that a very small proportion of people are capable of producing differential results—results that are not only significantly higher but significantly better as well. We then take on the responsibility for placing these people on the tasks where their specific strengths are likely to produce disproportionately large and disproportionately different results.

Managers need to realize that they are being paid for enabling people to do the work for which those people are being paid. It is the manager's job to ask anyone in the organization—first himself, then the boss, then the people who are his colleagues, and finally his subordinates—every six or nine months: "What do we in this organization do, and what do I do, that helps you in doing what you are being paid for? And what do we do, and what do I do, that hampers you?"

This should be asked of *everyone*. It is simply not true, as most managers assume, that they always understand how best to lay out routine work, whether machine-paced or clerical. Whenever we have asked: "What do we do that helps you in your work, and what do we do that hampers you?", we have found that there are a great many things that hamper and too few things that help.

For any but routine operations, the question is absolutely crucial. One has to assume, first, that the individual human being at work knows better than anyone else what makes him or her more productive, and what is helpful or unhelpful. One assumes, secondly, that to be fully productive, people of knowledge and skill need to take responsibility. It is the job of the boss to act as a resource and to support the motivation, the desire of people to do a job; for they know fully well what "productivity" for their work really means. Not to ask that question, in other words, quenches motivation. And even in routine work—as Taylor was the first to realize—the only true "expert" is the person who does the job.

The productivity of people requires, finally, continuous learning, as the Japanese have taught us. It requires that people are constantly challenged to think through what they can do to improve what they are already doing. It requires adoption in the West of the specific Japanese Zen concept of learning: that one learns in order to do better what one already knows how to do well.* To be sure, this presupposes enough psychological security in the work group so that people are not afraid of working themselves, or their colleagues and neighbors on the next machine or in the next office, out of a job. It requires commitment on the part of employers to anticipate redundancies and to train and place people. But above all, it requires willingness to ask employes systematically and to listen to their answers. It requires acceptance of the fact that the person who does the job is likely to know more about it than the person who supervises—or at least to know different things about it. This is particularly important for people who are putting knowledge and skill to work. By definition, the skilled worker must know more about his or her job and work than anybody else in the place, otherwise he/she is not adequately knowledgeable or adequately skilled.

Executives are, of course, aware that they have to manage productivities. But most of them believe this means finding the "trade-off" between a less productive and a more productive resource. Most executives—and many economists— believe, for instance, that managing productivities means substituting more productive capital equipment for more expensive and less productive labor, or vice versa.

There is little evidence that this "trade-off" ever really worked as a way to increase overall productivities. Few companies that installed computers to reduce the employment of clerks have realized their expectations; most computer users have found that they now need more, and more expensive, clerks even though they call them "operators" or "programmers." Similarly, the old fears that "automation" would result in large-scale unemployment have universally

---

* See my book *Management: Tasks, Responsibilities, Practices* (New York: Harper & Row, 1974; London: Wm. Heinemann, 1974).

been disproven; all automation might do is to shift employment from fairly low paid manual to much more highly paid technical or professional work. Both the computer and automation have often resulted in higher productivities, but not because of the alleged "trade-off." The careful productivity studies for which Simon Kuznets of Harvard received one of the earliest Nobel prizes in economics show something quite different. The rapid expansion of the American economy in the twentieth century did indeed rest on increasing capital investment, and especially on increasing productivity of capital. But employment went up as fast as capital investment. And wages, because of higher total productivity, went up much faster.

The substitution theory of productivity has thus always been suspect, despite its popularity. From now on, it will not work at all. From now on, all resources will have to be managed for greater productivity. Managers will have to assume that they cannot obtain greater overall productivity by trading a decrease in the productivity of one resource against an increase in another. Furthermore, they will have to assume that a decrease in the productivity of any one resource is likely to mean a decrease in overall productivity that cannot easily be offset.

Knowledge work, unlike manual work, cannot be replaced by capital investment. On the contrary, capital investment creates the need for more knowledge work. The first ones to find this out were the hospitals and universities. In the hospital, more capital investment does not result in saving labor; instead it creates demands for new and more highly paid labor. The expensive capital equipment needed for microsurgery, for kidney dialysis, or for intensive therapy to prevent shock, entails highly trained people. The unskilled work in the hospital has very largely been replaced by machinery; we have automated dishwashers, for instance. So the modern hospital needs only one-third the number of people per patient bed to clean floors and wash windows it used to employ in 1930. But the saving of labor in unskilled or semiskilled work has been more than offset by the increase in employment in skilled work created largely by heavy capital investment. The same thing has happened in the university. And the fact that these institutions, which fifty years ago were labor-intensive but not capital-intensive, are today both capital-intensive and labor-intensive, explains in large measure why the costs of health care and the costs of higher education have gone up disproportionately fast. Yet neither hospital administrator nor university administrator realized this until recently. Both believed that capital investment would "save labor," that in other words they would "trade off" "labor" against "capital." It did not work.

Even in manufacturing businesses, the trade-off of capital for labor has not always worked. One example is the paper industry. In 1929, one dollar of investment in papermaking produced around three dollars' worth of paper production per year. Capital was turned over productively about three times per year. By 1980, the productivity of capital in the paper industry had fallen to where it now takes three dollars of capital investment to produce one dollar's worth of saleable paper a year—one-ninth the productivity of capital of fifty years ago. But employment in the papermill, per ton of paper produced, is still two-fifths of what it was fifty years ago. In other words, while there has been a very sharp increase in the productivity of labor in papermaking as a result of large-scale mechanization, it has not been nearly as great as the decrease in the productivity of capital. The trade-off has not worked.

Steel mills had the same experience, as had the automotive plants. One of the reasons for Chrysler's troubles may have been the decrease in overall productivity resulting from unsuccessful—or less than successful—"trade-offs" of labor against capital investment. To be sure, the imminent shortage of people for traditional work will make automation increasingly attractive in the developed countries, and increasingly necessary. But unless at the same time the productivity of capital is significantly improved, the saving in labor will almost certainly turn out to be an illusion. And wherever "labor" means highly skilled people, knowledge people, managerial and professional people, there can be no such saving at all. There, the only way to increase productivity of "labor" is to increase the productivity of the people, that is, the productivity of time and the productivity of knowledge.

Managers thus have to manage separately the productivity of all four key resources: capital, crucial physical resources, time, and knowledge. But what matters in the end is the total, overall productivity of a specific institution in using its resources. What matters is the total overall productivity of this factory, this store, this bank, this hospital, this school, this office. It is the total overall productivity of all factors in a specific enterprise or institution that managers are being paid to promote. And it is the steady increase in the productivities of all resources in their specific institution to which managers must commit themselves in turbulent times.

The Costs of Staying in Business vs. the Delusion of Profit

Managing the fundamentals includes earning today the costs of staying in business tomorrow. A business that does not earn these costs is bound to fade and to disappear. These are not "future costs"; they are costs incurred now though not paid out until later. They are "accrued" or "deferred" costs—and we learned long ago that these are true costs that must be shown in the current accounts of a business. A business that does not earn the accrued costs of staying in business impoverishes the economy and is untrue to its first social responsibility: to maintain the wealth-producing and employment-producing capacities of the resources entrusted to the enterprise and its management.

"Profit," it cannot be said often enough, is an accounting illusion. Except in the rare case of the governmental monopoly, such as OPEC, there are no profits; there are only the deferred costs of staying in business. In the first place, capital is a resource. And there are, as by now we should all have learned, no "free" resources. The minimum cost of staying in business therefore is the cost of capital.

But economic activity by itself has deferred costs, costs of staying in business, which have to be earned today so that there is a business—or an economy—tomorrow. Economic activity can be defined as the commitment of present resources that are certain—the seed corn, to future expectations of a harvest. Future expectations always entail a risk, and a high risk; yet no economic activity is possible without the risk, just as no agriculture is possible without retaining part of the current harvest as the seed corn for next year. Economic advance means the ability to incur larger and more complex risks, to commit present resources to longer time periods and to the greater uncertainties of change and innovation. Economic advance thus depends on the ability of an economy to form capital, that is, to generate a surplus of current production over the costs of the past and present.

But economic advance also means the ability to substitute knowledge and skill for muscle and sweat. It means the creation of future jobs—both more jobs and better jobs. And this too depends, as we know, primarily on the rate of capital formation and on our ability to invest larger and larger sums in the creation of a future job. The more knowledge a job puts to work, the more capital investment does it require. It requires capital investment directly, in equipment and machinery— the quantum jump between the costs of a pencil and the costs of a hand-held calculator is one indicator of the jump in capital requirements per job. It requires even more capital indirectly in the form of high and rising investment in capital formation of the human resource, its schooling and education. Young graduate engineers in their early twenties just starting on their first jobs require in direct and indirect capital investment (in part made by the employer, in part by the family and by the taxpayer) about twenty-five times the capital investment that their grandfathers, the skilled carpenters, represented sixty years ago when they went to work on their first jobs after apprenticeship. And the engineer's son will probably require about five to ten times the total capital his father now requires. In other words, in all developed countries there is need for substantial scaling up of capital investment to provide tomorrow's jobs for today's young people and their expectations.

It is no longer sufficient to earn enough to cover the costs of the past and present. An enterprise does not "break even" when it covers the costs of the accounting model, the costs that have already been paid out. The costs of staying in business have already been incurred—they just have not been paid out. The amounts due cannot perhaps be established with the precision with which an accountant can determine what has already been paid out. But they can easily be determined within the range of probabilities and with the same margins of error that apply to the bulk of accounting figures, such as the valuation of fixed assets, of patents, or of outstanding claims. Indeed, the precision with which the costs of staying in business can be set is considerably higher than that for most figures in the conventional balance sheet and profit and loss statement. It has been an axiom of economics since the earliest work of the English economist Alfred Marshall, a hundred years ago, that in a market economy the costs of staying in business can never be lower than the costs of capital. An enterprise that earns less on the total amount of money in the business than the going rate for capital is by definition operating at a deficit and stealing from the future.

Everybody accepts this for the farmer who eats up the seed corn needed for next year's sowing. That we do not accept it in respect to business enterprise is, in large measure, the result of the delusion of "profit." Everyone knows that the farmer's seed corn is not profit, even though it is surplus. But no one—including business executives—grasps that the "profit" reported in company statements is not profit either; it is "seed corn." It is the "cost of staying in business"—an actual and genuine, albeit deferred, cost.

In turbulent times the need for capital formation is bound to go up, if only because turbulent times mean greater uncertainty and a higher risk premium on the committal of present and certain resources to the future. But we know that the times ahead are times of great change and innovation, socially and technologically—and this again means higher risks in the future. Finally, in all developed countries there is under way a sharp shift to skilled jobs requiring higher capital investment. In the developing countries the need ahead is for jobs—manufacturing jobs, mainly—that will require in their totality capital investments beyond any current imaginings, even if the investment in the individual job is still quite low.

At the same time, the impediments to capital formation are great and are getting greater. Capital formation in all developed countries is falling sharply. One reason is, of course, that inflation destroys capital. The public intuitively senses this, which explains why in an inflationary period people tend to increase their savings rate even though "common sense" would argue for shifting out of money and into things. The public senses, without benefit of economists, that it has to increase the sums laid aside in order to stay even with the declining value of its savings.

There are also structural and permanent changes that tend to depress the rate of capital formation in the developed countries, whether market economies or developed Communist countries. Fifty years ago, Keynes stood traditional economics on its head by showing that, under certain conditions, modern economies have a tendency toward "oversaving," so that capital formation needs to be discouraged and consumption encouraged. Now, because of structural changes in population,* we must expect in the developed countries a long period dominated by a chronic built-in tendency toward "under-saving" (the opposite of what Keynes diagnosed for his time but just as incompatible with classical economics). More and more personal savings, even in countries like Japan or Germany with their high personal savings rates, will not be "capital formation" at all but "delayed consumption."

To a large and increasing extent, in all developed countries, the bulk of personal savings are funds for retirement. Insofar as these funds are collected by government—as the largest part is everywhere, even in countries like the United States and Great Britain that have sizable private pension systems—they are "savings" only to the individual. They immediately become "spending" on the part of government. But most of what is being paid into private pension plans also goes out to pensioners, who spend by far the greatest part of it right away. The other major component of "personal savings" in developed non-Communist countries is investment in the individual family home. The home is a durable consumer good, albeit one that has a high resale value. It is not a "capital good" used to produce economic value or wealth. Investment in the home is not "capital formation." The more affluent a society becomes, and the more the broad masses become the sole recipients of national income through wages and salaries, the less do personal savings equate with capital formation. The more successful a society is in prolonging the individual

---

*On this see Part 3 below and also my book *The Unseen Revolution: How Pension Fund Socialism Came to America* (New York: Harper & Row, 1976; London: Wm. Heinemann, 1976).

lifespan, the lower inevitably is the rate of genuine capital formation by individuals.

There are other reasons for the drop in the rate of capital formation: the rapid increase in the current costs of doing business; the growth of governmental bureaucracies, which greatly increase the economy's cost burden; the growth in regulations; the increase of transfer payments (whether for the environment, for safety, or for goals of social policy). All these raise the cost of doing business and thereby impede the ability to earn the costs of staying in business. But the basic shift is structural, it is the shift in population structure and population dynamics. As a result of this shift, older people have become the largest-growing segment of the adult population, which sharply affects the savings rate. (See also Part 3 below.) This shift makes developed societies increasingly dependent for their capital formation on the ability of the organized non-governmental institutions—primarily businesses, of course—to earn the costs of staying in business, and thus to provide the "seed corn."

To most businessmen, as to most economists, this is obvious. There is therefore among businessmen and economists a growing concern with capital formation and a growing awareness of the inadequacy of the rate at which businesses today earn the costs of staying in business. But for the public, the politicians, the trade union leaders, and even for the senior people in organizations—let alone employes on all levels from the shop floor to such functional and technical areas as sales management or research—this obvious fact is totally invisible. It is obscured by the prevailing rhetoric of "profit." "Profit," we are told, is a "reward" to the investor. "Profit," we are told, is a return on what has been invested in the past. Nothing could be further from the truth. What is misleadingly labelled "profit" is genuine cost, the cost of the future of enterprise and economy. A rate of profit that does not equal the cost of capital is not "profit" at all. It is loss, both for the firm and for the economy.

Covering costs is surely a managerial responsibility. No one has ever argued otherwise. Managers thus have responsibility for earning the costs of staying in business.

One conclusion from this is that the "not-for-profit" institutions of the Third Sector—hospitals, universities, service organizations of all kinds—need to consider the cost of staying in business as a part of their operating costs. Today, these institutions treat a surplus of operating revenues over operating costs as a "profit" they are not supposed to make. They thereby conceal their true costs. But they also endanger their own future and impose burdens on society and on the wealth-producing capacity of the economy. This could be condoned as long as the Third Sector was marginal. But now the so-called Third Sector in most developed countries is far more than a "margin"; it accounts for at least one-fourth of national product. Today, we need to know how big the deficit of the Third Sector institutions really is.

The danger of treating the cost of staying in business as a "cost of the future" rather than as a cost of current operations in public service institutions is dramatically illustrated by the failure of the British National Health Service to account from 1950 until today for the known, ascertained, and measurable costs of needed hospital construction. The health service accounts were supposed to be "in balance" during most of these years, with the taxpayers paying the full costs. Actually, the service ran at a huge hidden deficit. As a result, there are today in many parts of the United Kingdom long and lengthening waiting periods for so-called elective surgery for those complaints where the disease itself does not get worse by postponing remedial action, though the patient suffers. Private health insurance has become the most popular and fastest-growing employe benefit in the United Kingdom. It does not pay for medical treatment or surgery; the health service does that. It pays for "jumping the queue." This, of course, is a straight denial of the very premise on which the National Health Service was founded. Indeed, the explosive growth of private health insurance in Great Britain bespeaks a basic failure of the National Health Service—an unnecessary failure, caused by nothing but the refusal to treat the costs of staying in business as legitimate costs, a refusal indeed to consider them as "costs" at all.

A deficit is a deficit, whether incurred by a soap maker, a university, a hospital, or the Boy Scouts. Managerially and entrepreneurially, these are very different institutions; economically, the only difference between them is the way the tax collector treats them. Many "not-for-profit" institutions ought to show what in traditional accounting would be treated as substantial "profits," that is, a substantial surplus of current income (whatever the source) over current outgo; in many service institutions the costs of staying in business are very high indeed. Universities and hospitals, both almost certain to undergo fairly drastic changes within the next decades, are good examples. As long, however, as the costs of staying in business, despite their certainty and measurability, are treated as "profit," the "not-for-profit" institutions of the Third Sector will not be managed for performance and service, but will indeed be mismanaged. We may choose to run many of these institutions on a subsidy from the tax-payers; others we may want to keep dependent on private charity. But the managements of these institutions owe it to themselves and to society to know how large the actual deficit is at which their institution is run—they owe it to themselves and to society to know their true costs, even if they are not expected to earn them.

For all managers, knowing the costs of staying in business and treating them as genuine costs is a basic responsibility.

This implies, first, that the financial figures of their institution be adjusted to inflation, so that managers know the true economic position of their enterprise. It implies, secondly, that managers accept that they operate at a loss *unless* the surplus of current revenues over costs of past and present covers the cost of capital for all the money employed in the business at current market rates. The cost of capital, to repeat, is always the minimum cost of staying in business.

It is moreover incumbent on managers to think through the costs of staying in business so as to provide for—or at least to identify—those costs that are likely or certain to exceed the going rate for the cost of capital. The costs of staying in business during the next few years are almost certain to be higher than the cost of capital for the hospital and the university, as has already been mentioned. But they are also certain to be a good deal higher for the traditional steel mills, for example, where high capital requirements for new processes and for automation coincide with demands for high environmental and safety investments and with capital demands for energy-conserving technologies. Until these costs are provided for out of current income, the enterprise has not "broken even."

There also is an urgent need to adjust executive compensation to economic reality. As long as executives get extra compensation based on reported "profits," they will resist changing the way they report their earnings. Extra compensation based on profits should never be paid until the costs of staying in business have been covered by current earnings. Not to disclose that the genuine costs, the costs of staying in business, have not been earned is fraud. To pay oneself "bonuses" based on a nonexistent profit is embezzlement.

But above all there is need to change the rhetoric and the use of totally misleading accounting figures. The costs of staying in business have to be reported to the stockholders, to the public, to the taxpayer. In their rhetoric, managers must emphasize increasingly the responsibility for earning the costs of risk, of change, of innovation, and of tomorrow's jobs for today's young people and the new entrants into the work force. They cannot do so unless they first make sure that the accounting figures of their own enterprises, by which they themselves manage, reflect reality rather than the delusion of "profit."

Next to the danger of falling productivities, the greatest danger to the world economy, and to the economy of every country in it, is the drop in capital formation. This drop is probably a good deal greater in the Communist countries than in the market economies, but again this is cold comfort. It is easier in a Communist country to increase the rate of capital formation, for the Communists have never talked about "profit," even though the surplus of current revenue over current costs on which Communist economies operate is many times the "profit margin" of market economies. (But the risks and uncertainties are also much higher in a centrally planned economy and the productivity of capital is very much lower.) The opposition to "profit" is growing in all countries, and as long as we try to explain it by such dubious rationalizations as the "profit motive"—for which there has never been a shred of evidence—or "reward to the investor," this resistance will grow. Unless managers make themselves see every time they look at their figures that there is no "profit," but only "costs of staying in business," they will continue to talk misleading nonsense—in the end it will, however, mislead no one but themselves. People sense that they are being duped.

In the United States the Securities Exchange Commission (SEC) has for the last few years tried to get accountants to estimate profits ahead. This is unlikely to work. Future revenues are always hard to estimate; in turbulent times, two or three years in the future, even the direction can be estimated with only a margin of error of plus or minus 50 percent. But the costs of staying in business can be estimated with high probability quite a few years out precisely because they are not "future costs" but "deferred costs." The SEC could make no greater contribution to the American economy and to the free economies all told than to demand of accountants that they estimate the costs of staying in business—with the cost of capital as the minimum—and include these as genuine costs in the published reports of the institutions whose accounts they audit and certify.

But the executive—whether in business or in a public service institution—had better not wait for SEC and accountants. He should start right now managing the costs of staying in business and treating them as genuine costs. Otherwise in turbulent and inflationary times he may well find that his enterprise sinks under the weight of real losses after reporting "record profits" year after year.

2

Managing for Tomorrow

Managing for Tomorrow

The fundamentals pertain to today's enterprise. But all institutions live and perform in two time periods: that of today and that of tomorrow. Tomorrow is being made today, irrevocably in most cases. Managers therefore always have to manage both today—the fundamentals—and tomorrow. In turbulent times, managers cannot assume that tomorrow will be an extension of today. On the contrary, they must manage for change; change alike as an opportunity and a threat.

Concentrating Resources on Results

In turbulent times the enterprise has to be kept lean and muscular, capable of taking strain but capable also of moving fast and availing itself of opportunity. This is particularly important if such times follow long years of comparative calm, ease, and predictability. Unless challenged, every organization tends to become slack, easygoing, diffuse. It tends to allocate resources by inertia and tradition rather than by results. Above all, every organization tends to avoid unpleasantness. And nothing is less pleasant and less popular than to concentrate resources on results, because it always means saying "No."

41

In turbulent times, any organization—business or public service institution—needs to control the assignment of its resources. It needs to think through where the results are likely to be. It needs to know the performing and productive resources within itself, and especially the performing and productive people. Organized, continuous, disciplined efforts are needed to commit these resources to actual and potential results. "Feed the opportunities and starve the problems" is the rule. And resources can be productive only if they are concentrated; fragmentation inhibits results.

One way to exercise assignment control and to concentrate is to have two budgets: an operational budget for the things that are already being done, and an opportunities budget for proposed new and different ventures. The operational budget will be much more voluminous than the opportunities budget, which even in a giant company rarely runs to more than a few pages. Yet both should be given the same amount of top management time and attention. The questions management asks of these two budgets are quite different. For the operational budget, one asks: "Is this effort and expenditure truly necessary? If not, how do we get out of it?" But if the answer is "Yes," one asks: "What is the *minimum* needed to prevent serious malfunction?" For the opportunities budget, the first question is: "Is this the right opportunity for us?" And if the answer is "Yes," one asks: "What is the optimum of efforts and resources this opportunity can absorb and put to productive use? And who is the right person to work on it?" The operational budget should always be funded on the lowest basis to get by. It should be "satisficed" rather than "optimized," to use the terms of formal decision theory. The opportunities budget should be optimized, i.e., funded to give the highest rate of return for efforts and expenditures.

But concentration of resources on results also requires a systematic commitment to what I would call "corporate weight control," or the abandonment of one less promising or less productive effort for every new effort taken on. This is particularly important for staff work, whether in personnel, marketing, research, or any other staff area. One should always ask the expert in the area: "What are you going to abandon so as to engage in this new activity?" As a rule, management should not sanction a new activity or effort in a staff area unless an old and less productive one is being sloughed off. For in staff efforts, only concentration of effort produces results. The rules of corporate weight control apply equally to new products, to additions to the product line, to additional distribution channels, and so on.

Sloughing Off Yesterday

After long years of relative calm and predictability, every enterprise—business or non-business public service institution—is likely to be loaded down with yesterday's promises. These include the products or services that no longer contribute; the acquisitions or ventures that looked so enticing when started, but now, five years later, still are only hopes; the intelligent ideas that failed to turn into performance; the products and services the need for which has disappeared with social or economic change; and the products and services that have made themselves obsolete by attaining their objectives. A ship that spends long periods of time at sea needs to be cleansed of its barnacles or their drag will deprive it of speed and maneuverability. An enterprise that has sailed in calm waters for a long time similarly needs to cleanse itself of the products, services, ventures that only absorb resources; the products, services, ventures that have become "yesterday."

Any enterprise needs such a systematic abandonment policy at all times, but especially in times of turbulence. Every product, every service—external and internal—every process, every activity needs to be put on trial every few years, with the question: "If we weren't in this already, would we go into it knowing what we *now* know?" And if the answer is "No," one does not say: "Let's make another study." One says: "How can we get out; or at least, how can we stop putting additional resources in?"

The time to ask these questions and to act upon the answers is not when the institution is in trouble. It is while it is successful. For then it is most likely to have its resources allocated to the past, to the things that *did* produce, to the goals that *did* challenge, to the needs that *were* unfulfilled.

Sloughing off yesterday is particularly important these days for the non-business public service institution. Its very success in a great many cases has made its programs, activities, services, obsolete and unproductive. But even abandonment of the failure, the unproductive, is difficult in service organizations. It is all but impossible for most of them to accept that success always means organizing for the abandonment of what has already been achieved. Service institutions are not *want*-oriented; they are *need*-oriented. By definition they are concerned with "good works" and with "social" or "moral" contributions rather than with returns and results. The social worker will always believe that the very failure of her efforts to get a family off welfare proves that more effort and more money are needed. She cannot accept that her failure—continuous and total over half a century—means that she had better stop doing what she is so valiantly failing in. The schoolmaster cannot accept that he has attained his age-old objective of getting all the children to attend school for long years, and that now he had better ask how to get more out of fewer years of schooling instead of continuing futile efforts to obtain even more years for even more students. The hospital considers it "unthinkable" that its efforts to improve childbirth have attained their objective to the point where "maternity" no longer belongs in a hospital for the sick, but in a "motel" with access to hospital services.

By and large, few service institutions attempt to think through the changed circumstances in which they operate. Most believe that all that is required is to run harder and to raise more money.

Precisely because results in service institutions are not easily measured, there is need for organized abandonment. There is need for a systematic withdrawal of resources— money, but above all, people—from yesterday's efforts. At the very least, the manager of a service institution should ask himself all the time how methods should be changed to accomplish what his institution originally set out to do.

But in businesses too, far too many executives look upon their products, services, activities as "good works," as a "moral duty" or something the Good Lord created, rather than as short-lived, human activities justifiable only if they produce results and satisfy a customer. Far too few businesses are willing to slough off yesterday, and as a result, far too few have resources available for tomorrow. In turbulent times, a business needs to be able both to outride sudden hard blows and to avail itself of sudden unexpected opportunities. For both, the concentration of resources on results and a sloughing off of the resource-devouring and unproductive past are primary requirements.

Managing Growth

Every business needs to manage growth. And to do so, it needs a growth strategy.

During the 1950s and 1960s, it was believed that everything has to grow and that there are no limits to growth. In the 1970s, it became popular to believe that growth is over forever. Both beliefs are fallacious.

Nothing can grow forever, let alone at an exponential rate. Yet every fifty years or so, since the early eighteenth century, the developed countries of the world economy have experienced a "go-go decade," a decade during which growth was everything and everything was supposed to be growing forever. The first of these was around 1710, with the South Sea Bubble and John Law's Louisiana schemes. The next was in the 1770s and 1780s. There was a "go-go decade" around 1830, and another one around 1870. The one around 1910 was aborted—at least in Europe—by World War I; in the United States it continued until 1929. And then we had the 1960s and 1970s.

Every one of these "go-go" periods was followed by a massive hangover, during which everybody believed that growth had stopped for good. It never did, and there is no reason to believe that it has stopped now.

But in every such period, growth shifts to new foundations. It then becomes important for a business to think through where the growth areas are for its specific strengths, and to shift its resources out of the areas in which results can no longer be achieved into those areas where the new opportunities can be found.

In every such period, obsolescence speeds up. And in turbulent times, an organized sloughing off of the past combined with a systematic concentration of resources are the first requirements of any growth policy.

In every such period it is important for a business, but also for a non-business public service institution, to decide just how much it has to grow so as not to become marginal in its market. For if one's market grows, one must grow with it—to be marginal means to become extinct.

Chrysler's policy offers a good example of what not to do. Around 1960 or so, the Chrysler automobile company decided in effect not to grow. It did not have the resources to grow from within. Its growth would therefore have required a merger, in all probability with a European company. Instead, Chrysler decided to remain "conservative" and to become "a factor" rather than "a leader" in the industry. This turned out to be a disastrous mistake. The automobile market grew fast, and by 1975 Chrysler had become marginal. Its very survival had become questionable, even with massive government help. In 1960 Volkswagen was a good deal weaker than Chrysler in all areas—financial, product, engineering, and marketing. But VW made the decision to grow with the market. It asked: "Where are the growth markets?" and concentrated on four of them: Continental Europe, Brazil, Mexico, and the United States. In those areas it tried to attain leadership. Chrysler, by trying to become a worldwide also-ran, only succeeded in becoming marginal.

A marginal institution always goes down disproportionately more whenever the economy goes down, and it comes up disproportionately less whenever the economy goes up. With every turn of the business cycle, it becomes weaker. And once a business has become marginal, it is exceedingly difficult to reverse this downward drift; in fact, it is almost impossible.

The term "marginal" in this context is a matter of industry structure. It means something very different in hotels from what it means in the chemical industry. Industry structures also change. Thirty years ago, it was quite possible to be number two in the electrical apparatus industry within a major national market. Westinghouse in the United States and AEG in Germany then had a perfectly tenable position as number two producers within their markets. Today, one has to be among the small group of leaders on the world market. Maybe alone among electrical industry executives Sir Arnold Weinstock in the United Kingdom understood this. The British General Electric Company, which he built up in the sixties and seventies largely by merging a number of weak and marginal enterprises and by ruthlessly dropping all areas in which the company could not obtain leadership, has become a viable business. Companies that were much bigger and much stronger when he began—such as Westinghouse in the

United States—have since drifted and become successively less profitable, less able to compete.

A minimum amount of growth may thus be necessary to survival. It is always necessary if the market is growing or if the industry structure is changing.

A business needs to distinguish between the wrong kind of growth and the right kind of growth, between muscle, fat, and cancer. The rules are simple: Any growth which, within a short period of time, results in an overall increase in the total productivities of the enterprise's resources is healthy growth. It should be fed and supported. But growth that results only in volume and does not, within a fairly short period of time, produce higher overall productivities is fat. A certain amount of fat may be needed; but few businesses suffer from too little fat. Any increase in volume that does not lead to higher overall productivity should be sweated off again. Finally, any increase in volume that leads to reduced productivities, except for the shortest of start-up periods, is degenerative if not pre-cancerous. It should be eliminated by radical surgery—fast.

Managing Innovation and Change

In technology, as in economics, the twenty-five years from the Marshall Plan to the early seventies were years of extremely rapid growth and development—and yet they were also years of continuity. The most important feature of the technology of the postwar period was not innovation; it was the extension of modern technology to all parts of the world as a consequence of the penetration during World War II of the most remote corners by modern armies with modern armaments and modern methods. Lhasa in Tibet is still not listed among the world's commercial airports, but it is the exception. And even in Lhasa, I suspect, there are people now who have television sets though the surrounding mountains would seem to bar electronic signals. Apart from such remote corners as Tibet, the highlands of Bolivia, Albania, or the jungles of the Amazon, there is hardly any place in the world today that cannot be reached by telephone; no place where people need to be told what the mushroom cloud in the movie or on the television screen means; no place where movie and radio have not penetrated and transformed lives far more drastically than the railroad transformed the lives of people in the nineteenth century.

The Indian government is pursuing a policy of "Small is beautiful," and believes that "Gandhi's one major mistake was to push the spinning wheel." Yet to a visitor driving through the Indian villages, the pervading impression is not of an age-old poverty, age-old disease, and age-old misery. It is, rather, the brand-new bicycles outside each miserable hovel. It is the transistor radio which, turned on full blast, blares from every passing bullock cart, every camel cart, every elephant howdah. It is the crowds at the village markets who stand ten-deep around stores that offer motorbikes or small tractors or television sets even though there is as yet no television reception in the area.

But while the penetration of technology accelerated greatly during the twenty-five postwar years, technology itself largely continued along paths that had been laid out earlier. The "new technologies" of the fifties, sixties, and seventies were in the main based on science and knowledge that had been produced before World War I, and certainly before 1929. Two major exceptions are the computer, even though many of its basic concepts and technologies were largely developed in the twenties and computer technologies of later vintage are only now beginning to have substantial impact. And in medicine the "miracle drugs" of the 1950s and 1960s, which go back to work done as late as the forties during World War II.

In the twenty-five years after World War II, a continuous refrain was the acceleration in the speed of technological change. But this was largely a misunderstanding. What actually accelerated was the awareness of technological change. Technological change itself probably did not speed up at all; it may even have slowed down. Certainly there was nothing between 1945 and 1975 comparable to the technological changes of the sixty years between 1856 and World War I. These began with the discovery of the first synthetic dye, the design of the first working dynamo and of the typewriter; they ended with the first powered flight by the Wright Brothers, with Lee DeForest's audion tube, and with symbolic logic, which provided the basic concepts for electronics and data processing, including the very concept of "data." During that sixty-year period a new invention, leading almost immediately to a new industry, was made on average every fourteen to eighteen months. In the period between 1947 and 1975, only two truly new industries emerged: computers and systemic drugs, beginning with the sulfas of the late thirties and the antibiotics of the forties.

The next twenty or twenty-five years are almost certain to be more akin to the years before 1914 than to those between 1947 and 1975. It is fashionable nowadays to believe that technological change has come to an end—and indeed to believe that it is not desirable and can be stopped. This is not new; it is the common reaction in a period of rapid technological change. It was the reaction of the 1830s, when the Luddites, the machine wreckers, were far more visible than the innovators. It was the reaction of the 1890s, the last period of disenchantment with technology in Western history. But just as the Luddites and the technological pessimists of the nineties made no lasting impact, so, it can be said, will today's romantic objection to technology remain ineffectual. It can cause serious dislocation. The fear of new technology of the generation of H. G. Wells in 1890 seriously crippled Great Britain and ensured that she would stick to the old technologies of the nineteenth century, falling behind in the science-based technologies of the twentieth century. But it did not impede, nor even slow down, the worldwide spread and advancement of technology. It only shifted technology, and with it economic leadership, to new areas. This is also the only possible result of the outcry against tomorrow's technologies in today's developed countries.

It is popularly believed that the lead time between new knowledge and its conversion into products and services has recently become much shorter. Not so. The lead time is today what it has been for a very long time, about thirty to forty years.

Werner Siemens invented the first practicable dynamo in 1856. Twenty-two years later, in 1878, Thomas Edison designed the electric light bulb, which made electricity an effective technology. A few years later Westinghouse developed the alternating current motor, which made electricity the prime mover for industrial production. William Henry Perkins, in 1856, had discovered the first synthetic aniline dye made from coal tar. But it was not until 1880 that the Germans, picking up Perkins's fundamental discovery, developed the modern dyestuff industry. The main-frame computer was developed as a practical machine in 1945, at the very end of World War II. Thirty years later, in the mid-seventies, with miniprocessor, integrated circuits, and ordinary-language logic, the computer first became an everyday tool.

On the basis of this thirty- to forty-year lead time, the period of fundamental technological changes is ahead of us. Unlike the quarter century after World War II, it will be a period of structural change rather than one of modification, of extension, or of exploitation. The period ahead will shift technological change to new realms.

One of these areas of structural change ahead is electronics. The fundamental scientific knowledge was produced in the late thirties and early forties. The 1980s are therefore almost certain to be a period of high technological impact and true innovation.

A major impact is going to be in communications. Until now, electronic communication has largely adapted itself to the traditional definition of voice, vision, and graphics as distinct separate kinds of communication. From now on, electronics will increasingly produce total communications. By the middle of 1980 the Business Communications Satellite (a joint venture of IBM, Xerox, and the American satellite company Comsat) should be in operation in the United States. It will make possible simultaneous and instantaneous electronic transmission of voice, of vision, and of graphics (such as documents or charts). This will enable people in twenty-five places anywhere on the face of the globe to be in one visual place where they can talk to each other directly, see each other, and if need be share the same reports, the same documents, the same graphs simultaneously, without leaving their own office or home. The equivalent communications capacity is available in a number of different systems—for instance, in the new telephone exchanges that are being pioneered by the British Post Office and by competitors to the Bell Telephone System in the United States.

As a result, business travel on the airlines has probably passed its peak. Such travel was one of the growth industries of the post-World War II period. It should increasingly become less important, although its place may well be taken (and taken with a vengeance) by travel for vacation, learning, and sheer curiosity, defined as non-business travel. But business travel should become less and less necessary. It will be possible for executives to get together without moving that heavy, inert object, the human body, and inflicting upon it stupefying hours of vibration in stale air. Increasingly, we will be able to meet "in person" without having to move the person.

An equal or more important change will be the ability to substitute electronic transmission of graphics for the shipping of heavy paper. Marshall McLuhan made the headlines in the sixties by predicting that the electronic "message" would replace the old traditional "medium," the printed word, the graphic information. This has not happened and it will not happen. On the contrary, electronics are becoming the main channel for the transmission of graphic, printed information. Until today, we had to put a few grains of ink on half a pound of heavy cellulose through a printing process, and then to transport the inert mass of cellulose over long distances, to be finally hand-carried to the individual audience, slowly and at great cost. But today almost everyone has two printing plants in his home, the telephone and the television set. The telephone (already used by the British Post Office to transmit graphics) is easy, cheap, and a two-way channel. Its graphic quality, however, is poor and likely to remain so. The television set, on the other hand, has excellent graphics; the video cassette has already better graphic quality than most commercial printing presses. So far, the television set allows only one-way communication. Nevertheless, between the two tools we have a complete system for transmitting graphics, which will reach into practically every household in the developed countries. The remaining obstacles are not technical or economic, but legal and political. Electronic transmission of graphics is infinitely cheaper, let alone infinitely faster, than the traditional methods, which could be justified only as long as there were no alternatives. Within twenty to twenty-five years, it can be predicted with high confidence, the bulk of what we call newspapers and magazines today will be transmitted through electronics and through the printing plant of a telephone or television set.

We can also anticipate major technological changes in the field of health care. The new knowledge developed from the early thirties until the fifties, when Crick and Watson deciphered the genetic code, will lead to the development of bioelectronics and biogenetics to complement biochemistry and biomechanics (or surgery), and to the development of artificial organs that the body does not reject. There is the genetic manipulation of the chromosomes in the cell. And there is biogenetics, which uses the body's own dynamics to change or correct organic defects and deficiencies, whether genetic or the result of metabolic malfunction. These new technologies will not replace traditional medicine; they will complement it. But they bid fair to blur the age-old distinction between "internal medicine" and "surgery." Unlike internal medicine, they constitute invasions of the body; yet, unlike surgery, they are likely to be bloodless, and will mobilize the body's own forces for corrective action.

Well before 1995, the "modern" manufacturing technology of the twentieth century, the "assembly line," will largely have disappeared, to be replaced by true automation. All along, the "assembly line" was a temporary compromise rather than a permanent solution, and poor engineering to boot. It did not use the strengths of the human being but, instead, subordinated human strengths to the requirements of the machine. In fact, the assembly line—despite its high visibility and symbolic importance—never employed more than a very small fraction of people. At its peak around World War II, maybe 5 to 8 percent of the American labor force employed in manufacturing worked on the "assembly line." Many more, of course, work on assembly, and are likely to continue to do so. But most assembly is not "assembly line." The workers, for instance, who put together a radio or television set, a computer or an airplane, do not work on an "assembly line," even though they work on "assembly." They do a complete job at their own rhythm and their own speed, largely independent of what anybody else on the floor is doing. In areas in which we can use the specific strengths of human beings— their ability to do a large number of different operations, to do them at different rhythms and different speeds, and to exercise judgment—automation has little to offer. But where there is an "assembly line," where human beings are used or misused as if they were parts of a machine, true automation is infinitely superior. The numerically controlled machine tool that has programmed, computerized instruction built into it will make the "assembly line" rapidly obsolete. For the numerically controlled tool can do the one thing the assembly line cannot do: it can change what is being produced, and to a large extent how it is being produced, without confusion and without extremely expensive machine downtime. By the end of this century the "assembly line," at least in developed countries, will have become history.

Altogether, within ten or fifteen years we will see a development as important as the integration of the electrical motor into the individual machine at the end of the nineteenth century. Any photograph of a manufacturing plant, a retail store, or even an office around 1900 shows the pulleys, belts, or treadles that brought power to the machines. By 1930 the production of power had become part of the machine itself. Sewing machines were driven by pedal power until 1930; since then, they have had electric motors. Spindles in the textile factory received power from a central source as late as 1925; every spindle produced since then has its own small electrical motor. Typewriters followed in 1950—only older people or college kids use "manual" typewriters today; everybody else uses a typewriter with an electric motor.

From now on, information and control will increasingly be embodied in the machine. Increasingly, the computer (as in the form of a miniprocessor) will be as much a part of the productive tool as the electric motor became in the last seventy-five years. Medical and testing instruments will have their own built-in processors and controls—whether in health care, in the factory, at the airport, or in the airplane aloft. The integration of information processing and information analysis with the operating tool is, in its way, as radical a change as was the integration of prime energy producer and machine tool at the close of the nineteenth and the opening of the twentieth century. And it will take less time.

The new information technology may transform banking, too. Banking for the consumer, which is primarily focused on transactions and information, may become a major industry, separate from the banking serving business and industry. Sears, Roebuck—America's retail giant—has already begun to buy up Savings and Loan associations (a form of consumer finance institution), and is forging them into a national chain focused on the needs of the American family. The banking needs of business—and especially of transnational business—may, however, be totally different, in respect to information and to financial services alike. The "universal bank" of yesterday, the bank that offered financial services to every kind of client—retail or family customer; commercial customer; large corporation—may well split into different, highly specialized and separate, if not independent, institutions, each of which melds information and financial services in different ways.

The examples given above are not a listing but a sample. What is clear is that the tremendous amount of new knowledge produced in the last thirty years since the end of World War II is now beginning to have an impact on technology. Knowledge is becoming performance, and this means rapid change. The technological change is only a part of the story; social change and social innovation should be equally important. It is highly possible that we can anticipate a period of rapid change in a great number of areas, regardless of the attitude of the public toward technological change. Resistance to change may make it more expensive but is unlikely to slow it down. Resistance to change may mean that economic leadership tomorrow passes from old to new countries, and from old to new industries. In the late nineteenth century Great Britain lost her leadership, which passed to Germany and the United States. And in the period after World War II the Japanese, precisely because they were in many ways technologically backward, could gain leadership in an area that traditional Western industry had largely neglected—high-technology consumer goods. Such shifts may happen again, are indeed likely to happen again. But this does not alter the fact that technology is changing rapidly and that innovation, both technological and social, is speeding up and is likely to change the structure of economy and society.

The change furthermore is likely to lead to alterations in the economical size needed for effective operations. In some industries, the optimum size may go up; in others it may go down. Traditionally, there has been a premium on being small in innovation. Large organizations successful in yesterday's technologies tend to be defensive rather than offensive. But tomorrow's technologies may require very large capital investment at a fairly early stage. Communication systems, for instance, are by definition large systems.

In other areas optimal sizes may become much smaller. The steel industry of the world is in severe crisis, we are told. But this is not true of the "mini-mills" using the direct reduction method to convert scrap into new steel. With the enormous quantities of steel produced in the world over these last twenty or thirty years, there is now so much scrap available that tomorrow's steel needs can largely be met by reusing yesterday's steel product instead of smelting newly mined iron ore. But the mini-mills, which make steel from scrap rather than from ore, are pygmies compared to the traditional integrated steel mill.

In different industries the economic size of operation may thus go in different directions. Potential new technologies to develop new sources of energy—whether by the gasification or liquefication of coal, the development of hydrocarbons from oil shale or tar sands, or large-scale solar energy or wind energy systems—require giant size and huge investments. But in energy, too, very small units may emerge, such as solar energy collectors for the individual house.

In publishing, one trend is clearly toward very large systems: a national or worldwide system for the electronic communication of graphics would be very big indeed. At the same time, the conversion of every telephone or television set into a printing plant offers unlimited opportunity for a truly small publication, such as the specialized magazine for the beekeeper that cannot count on more than 10,000 subscribers in the United States, and maybe not more than 25,000 worldwide. If transmitted over the television set, such a magazine might well become economically viable. To take the example of banking again, we might well go both ways. The leading regional bank that has proven the success story of the last thirty years—the Swiss banks, or Cleveland Trust Company in the United States—might well prove to be the wrong size tomorrow. But at both extremes there will be opportunities: for the truly "world-class" bank, which can offer all banking and information services worldwide; and for the highly specialized, primarily local, financial institution (one example of this is the leasing companies that have blossomed during the last thirty years). This may also be true in the fields of health care and especially of education. We may face a period in which there are economies of very large scale and economies of very small scale, but none of medium scale.

In the past, new industries have rarely grown from existing old ones. The new industries of the last thirty years have primarily been developed by companies that either did not exist at all before World War II or were unknown and inconspicuous then. IBM, for instance, was a tiny company as late as 1939, when it had only a few millions in sales and had just hired its first engineer. As late as 1950, IBM looked like the least likely company to succeed in the computer field. It had little technical or scientific expertise and not too much market standing either. The old electrical companies— General Electric, Radio Corporation of America, Westinghouse—seemed certain "winners." In Europe too the computer "winners" seemed likely to be such old-established companies as Siemens, AEG, or Phillips. But IBM, largely because it was not encumbered by the past, became the leader in the computer field.

Of all the great chemical companies of the pre-World War II period, only one, Hoechst, has today a leading position in the new pharmaceutical fields that opened up in the forties. The other leaders of today, Hoffman-La Roche, Pfizer, or Merck, were small companies as late as 1950.

It is reasonable to suggest that many of the giants of tomorrow will be companies that either do not exist today or are so small as to be almost invisible. Yet, paradoxically, the innovations of tomorrow will have to come out of existing large companies far more than at earlier periods. One reason is the escalation of capital needs. The amount of money needed to make a fundamental invention is probably the same. But the amount of money, time, and effort needed to develop an invention into a product or service, let alone a new industry, is many times greater than it used to be. There is also a greater need, especially in the development phase, for people of substantial specialized skills; such people are found largely in existing large companies.

We must therefore learn how to make the existing companies, and particularly large companies, capable of innovation. We need a strategy that will enable existing businesses first to identify the opportunities for innovation and then to give effective leadership in such innovation. It will no longer be sufficient to extend existing technologies, to broaden them, modify them, or attempt to adapt them. From now on, the need will be to innovate in the true sense of the word, to create truly new wealth-producing capacity, both technical and social.

"Innovation" does not necessarily mean research, for research is only one tool of innovation. Innovation means, first, the systematic sloughing off of yesterday. It means, next, the systematic search for innovative opportunities—in the vulnerabilities of a technology, a process, a market; in the lead time of new knowledge; in the needs and wants of the market. It means the willingness to organize for entrepreneurship, to aim at creating new businesses rather than new products or modifications of old products. It means, finally, the willingness to set up the innovative venture separately, outside the existing managerial structure, to organize proper accounting concepts for the economics and control of innovation, and appropriate (very different) compensation policies for innovators. In the period ahead, the old-established companies will only succeed—or even survive—if they can set up their innovation as a major distinct business, and if they can commit themselves alike to a systematic sloughing off of yesterday's entrepreneurial attitude and to the financial and managerial organization that innovation requires.

It is only reasonable to assume that the turnover in the ranks of big business will be high. Even in highly stable times, such as the twenty-five years between the Marshall Plan and the early seventies, about one-half of the "Fortune Five Hundred" turned over within a generation, some 250 of them either disappearing altogether or dropping out of the front ranks. In turbulent times, economic metabolisms are certain to speed up. But the large company that organizes for innovation will have an advantage; it will have the resources of people and capital needed for such innovation in the present technological and market conditions.

Business Strategies for Tomorrow

During the last twenty-five or thirty years, the concept of "planning" proved highly productive. One could assume a continuation of trends within fairly narrow ranges, rather than sudden sharp shifts. One could start out with today and project it into the future—which is what businessmen, politicians, and economists alike usually mean by "planning." One could assume that tomorrow would continue today, with a different "mix" perhaps but much the same basic configuration.

The most probable assumption today is the unique event, which changes the configuration drastically.

Unique events cannot be "planned." They can, however, be foreseen, or rather, one can prepare to take advantage of them. One can have *strategies* for tomorrow that anticipate the areas in which the greatest changes are likely to occur, strategies that enable a business or public service institution to take advantage of the unforeseen and unforeseeable. Planning tries to optimize tomorrow the trends of today. Strategy aims to exploit the new and different opportunities of tomorrow.

Any institution needs to think strategically what its business is doing and what it should be doing. It needs to think through what its customers pay it for. What is "value" for *our* customers? This question, it should be emphasized, is as important for the public service not-for-profit institution (whether hospital or university, trade association or the Red Cross) as it is for a business. Every institution needs to think through what its strengths are. Are they the right strengths for its specific business? Are they adequate? Are they deployed where they will produce results? And what specifically is the "market" for this particular business, both at the present time and in the years immediately ahead?

Typically, businesses—but even more, non-profit public service institutions—believe that a strategy that aims at "a happy medium" is most comfortable, least risky, and adequately profitable. They are wrong. In many markets one prospers only at the extremes: either as one of the few market leaders who set the standard, or as a specialist supplying a narrow range of products or services, but with such advantage in knowledge, service, and adaptation to specific needs as to be in a class of one's own. The in-between position is rarely desirable or even viable.

During the last few years, the Boston Consulting Group has gained wide publicity for its theory that large sales volume and market penetration are by themselves disproportionately profitable. This is only partly in accord with the evidence. What is profitable is either market leadership in a broad market or to be a specialist preempting a narrow ecological niche. And what "market leadership" means is a matter of industry and market structure rather than of sales volume, something that varies widely in different markets.

In the world's automobile industry one can survive and prosper as one of a very small number of worldwide automotive companies, each of which essentially covers the entire range. But one can no longer survive, as Chrysler tried to do, as the number three in the U.S.—even though Chrysler as said earlier had the sales volume. Yet it is possible, indeed profitable, to be a specialist occupying a specific fairly small niche in that market, to produce, say, Jeeps or Rolls-Royces. It is the in-between position, which Chrysler planned for, that is not truly tenable any more. The in-between companies that aimed at being leaders in regional markets are becoming increasingly marginal.

The field of book publishing is quite different again. Book publishing is not a "world market" business, if only because of the language barrier. There is no high premium on size or sales volume though a publisher needs access to a distribution system so that very small size may be heavily penalized. Book publishing rests on the personal relationships of an editor with a number of authors, and no editor can work with a very large number. This gives book publishing a minimum economic size but does not give the large publisher much of an advantage. Beyond the minimum size the large publisher may even be penalized because larger size may make a publisher less attractive to his primary customer, the author. But there are also "specialists" in publishing, the publishers of large numbers of learned monographs, each selling only a few hundred copies but marketed with a minimum of distribution expense to a clearly defined worldwide specialty audience— Springer in Germany, for instance, Elsevier in Holland, or Westview in the United States.

Public service institutions may similarly find themselves confronted with new size specifications. In the U.S., for instance, the small, denominational college has proven remarkably strong as a specialist these last ten years. It can confine itself successfully to a narrow range of offerings, can concentrate its resources on eight or ten disciplines, and within those can offer the advantages of a small school in which the student has a "home." Students and faculty know each other, and there is a sense of high discipline, heightened *esprit de corps*, and a common dedication to fundamentals of religion, morality, and learning. At the other end of the scale is a very large, and steadily growing, minimum size, which for the traditional undergraduate college today may lie around 2,500 students. It is thus becoming increasingly doubtful whether the typical "good" undergraduate college—the Oberlin, the Pomona, the Carleton—can really survive. For that type of college which cannot opt, as the small denominational school does, for a very narrow range of subject matters, large size plus access to a graduate school that offers integrating and advanced work in such areas as the languages, mathematics, the performing arts, the graphic arts, and the sciences, may be a prerequisite for survival. But there may also be an upper limit to the optimal size in higher education in America. Above 8,000 or 10,000 students there are no more economies of scale and increasing diseconomies. Administrative overhead goes up faster than student enrollment, let alone revenues. In other words, the structure of American higher education is one in which "market leadership" is a qualitative term and quantities are primarily restraints, both in terms of minimum and optimum size.

The same applies to the hospital. The minimum economical size for the American hospital may today be around two hundred beds. But there is also an upper optimal size, around eight hundred beds or so, above which a hospital becomes only more expensive, not more effective.

"Industry leadership" is thus a matter of quality and of concentration on areas of strength, rather than of size alone. For as the example of the denominational college indicates, there is room in almost every area for the true "specialist" who preempts a small ecological niche.

Typical is a company in the pharmaceutical industry that systematically looks for products which, without scientific or technological dimension, will give it a leadership position in an area that is so small as not to be worthwhile for the large companies. The first product of this company was an enzyme that enables the eye surgeon to perform cataract surgery a little faster and with some slight improvement in the risk of failure. The scientific contribution was small—not much more than a longer shelf-life for the enzyme. But once the product was on the market, there was no point whatever in anyone else competing. The large pharmaceutical companies could only have beaten down the price had they entered the market.

Either strategy—market leadership or what we call "tollgate" specialization—can succeed. What is not tenable is the strategy in between. The strategy that tries to combine both almost never works. The two areas require different behavior, offer different rewards, and suit different temperaments. It is, however, possible and often advantageous to combine a number of separate, small ecological niches in one business—each aimed at a specific market, each aimed at a specific specialization, each preempting a separate "tollgate" position.

Any business needs to know its strengths and to base its strategy on them. What do *we* do well? What are the areas in which *we* perform? Most businesses and public service institutions alike believe it possible to be a "leader" in every area. But strengths are always specific, always unique. One gets paid only for strengths; one does not get paid for weaknesses. The question, therefore, is first: "What are our specific strengths?" And then: "Are they the right strengths? Are they the strengths that fit the opportunities of tomorrow, or are they the strengths that fitted those of yesterday? Are we deploying our strengths where the opportunities no longer are, or perhaps never were? And finally, what additional strengths do we have to acquire? What performance capacities do we have to add to exploit the changes, the opportunities, the turbulences of the environment—those created by demographics, by changes in knowledge and technology, and by the changes in the world economy?"

In thinking through its strategy, a business needs to study both concentration and diversification. We know what kinds of institutions produce results. The most profitable businesses over long periods of time are single-product businesses in the right product, the IBMs or GMs. The least profitable businesses over long periods are single-product businesses with the wrong product—typically the traditional steel industry in developed countries. But businesses diversified around a core of unity and especially around market unity are as profitable and successful as single-product businesses in the right products. Typical in the United States is Johnson & Johnson, a company that is widely diversified, with businesses ranging in technological complexity from producing a standard commodity, cotton gauze, to advanced birth control products. But all are consumer health-care products that go to the same market and through the same distribution channel, the drugstore.

And as unprofitable, over the long run, as the single-product business that is in the wrong product are the conglomerates—businesses that are diversified without a core of unity, whether in market or technology. It is possible, indeed profitable, to be an "intelligent investor" who holds dominant positions in a very small number of different businesses. One example of this is the English Pearson group, which holds controlling interests in a number of businesses: newspaper and magazine publishers, a major merchant bank, a construction company, and so on. Flick in Germany also belongs as such an example, with controlling holdings in half a dozen companies in Germany and the United States; as does Thomas Tilling in England or the American Mellons in Pittsburgh. The investors concentrate on a small number of businesses so that they can pay attention to each. They have a large enough share in these businesses to have veto power. They work at their investments. They take part in crucial decisions, and make sure that their businesses think through their policies, objectives, and strategies. They make sure that their businesses have first- rate managements. But the businesses are not managed by them, but by autonomous professional managements.

A "conglomerate," on the other hand, being an assembly, under one management, of a wide diversity of businesses without a common core of unity, cannot expect superior results and performance in the long run, and especially not in turbulent times.

Trouble is predictable sooner or later. There also is a high premium on knowing and understanding the business, which is not just obtained by financial analysis but needs the temperamental empathy one develops by experience, in a given fairly narrow area, by constant exposure to the qualitative aspects of an industry, a technology, or a market.

Yet every "right" product sooner or later becomes the "wrong" product. Every product sooner or later becomes a "commodity." Every product ages and eventually becomes obsolete. No product can expect to be the "right" product for more than thirty or forty years. IBM is clearly at the point where its product is becoming the "wrong" product. Even the American Telephone Company, despite the intelligent management of its monopoly position, is now at the point where its product is becoming the "wrong" product. Then a business has to diversify.

One of the critical strategy decisions is therefore when to diversify and how. A determination to diversify too early, when a single product or product line is still the right product, could jeopardize one's leadership. But to wait too long would jeopardize one's survival.

A Scorecard for Managers

"Management audits" are hotly debated these days by business's friends and by its critics, by regulatory agencies, in management seminars and in management journals. The proponents usually argue for a searching inquiry into basic management qualities: a management's morale and integrity, its creativity, its "social values," its human empathy, and so on. "Nonsense," the opponents retort; "the only thing that counts is performance, and that is measured by the bottom line."

Both sides, it can be said unequivocally, are wrong. There is a need to appraise management. It is even likely that within a fairly short time boards of directors will have the legal duty to appraise the management of publicly held companies. But it is equally true that only performance can be appraised. The things that the proponents of "management audits" talk about—integrity or creativity, for instance—are better left to the novelist.

Yet the "bottom line" is not an appropriate measure of management performance either. The bottom line measures business performance rather than management performance. And the performance of a business today is largely a result of the performance, or lack of it, of earlier managements in years past.

Today's executives are, of course, a good deal more than passive custodians of the past. They can modify the decisions they inherited. In fact, to bail out these decisions when they go wrong, as decisions in respect to the future are likely to do, is one of their most important and most difficult assignments. But today's executives also are charged with the responsibility for making the future of the business, with lead times that are becoming ever longer and in some areas range beyond ten years.

Performance in management, therefore, means in large measure doing a good job of preparing today's business for the future. This is where the measurement of management performance—or at least an appraisal of it—is needed the most, especially in turbulent times.

The future of a business is largely formed by present management performance in four areas: in each of these areas the performance average of management can be shown. In each, management can greatly improve its performance once it knows the record.

1. *Performance in appropriating capital:* Almost every company has elaborate procedures for capital appropriations. In companies in which divisional managers have virtually complete freedom, top management still reserves to itself the final decision on even fairly small capital investments. Most managements spend an enormous amount of time on capital appropriation decisions, but few pay much attention to what happens after the capital investment has been approved. In many companies there is no way of even finding out. To be sure, if the new multimillion dollar plant gets behind schedule or costs a great deal more than was originally planned, everybody knows about it. But once a plant is on stream, its performance is rarely compared with the expectations that led to the investment. And smaller investments,

though in their totality equally important, are barely looked at once a decision has been made.

Yet there are few better tests of the competence and performance of a management than its performance in appropriating capital and the actual results of capital investment decisions measured against expectations. General Motors has known this for about fifty years; its system for monitoring the performance of managerial capital investment decisions was first published in 1927.

We need to measure first the return on the investment itself against the return expected when the investment decision was made, and then the impact of the investment decision on the return and profitability of the entire business, again against the expectations at the time the decision was made. To organize this feedback from the results of capital appropriation decisions is fairly simple. It does not, except in the biggest and most complex companies, require a computer run, but can be done on a spread sheet. The key components are a willingness to commit oneself to expectations when the decision is being made, and the intellectual honesty to face up to the actual results.

2. *Performance in people decisions:* Everyone agrees that the development and placement of managerial and professional people is the ultimate control of any organization. This is the only way to make sure that today's decisions will bear fruit. By their very nature, decisions made with respect to the future, i.e., managerial decisions to commit today's economic resources to future uncertainty, will run into difficulties. And then one must depend on the ability of tomorrow's people to bail out today's decisions. Yet, while admitted to be crucial, this area is usually considered to be "intangible." But neither what is expected of a person's performance when he or she is put into the job, nor how the appointment works out, is "intangible." Neither can be quantified, but both can be fairly easily judged.

One thing we can be sure of when an appointment does not turn out as well as expected is that the executive who made the decision, who selected and appointed the person, made the wrong decision or—to put it differently—made the decision the wrong way. To blame a promotion that fails on the promoted person, as is usually done, is no more rational than to blame a capital investment that has gone sour on the money that was put into it. Executives who know how one makes decisions about people and who work on such decisions do not blame their appointees. They blame themselves. Few, very few, of the men they pick for promotions turn out to be incompetent. These executives never believe that good decisions are made by "good judges of people." They know that they are made by human beings who work on such decisions, and especially by executives who make sure that they check how the people they have chosen actually work out in practice.

It is not easily possible to assess, let alone to test scientifically, the spirit of an organization and the development of the people in it. But it is quite easy to test the results of that spirit and development, in other words, to assess the performance of decisions made about people, compared to the expectations underlying them. All it needs is a "scorecard" that judges results against expectations.

3. *Performance in innovation:* What was expected from a research effort, from a development effort, from a new business or a new product? And what are the actual results— one year, two, three, five years later? Research results cannot be predicted or projected forward, we are told all the time. But they can be measured, or at least appraised, and then projected backward on the promises and expectations at the time the research effort was started. The same thing is equally true of development efforts, of a new business, a new product, a new market, and of innovation altogether.

Even the most competent management probably bats, at best, around 0.300 in the innovation area, with one real success for every three tries. Innovation is chancy. But surely there is a reason, other than luck, why some managements, such as Procter & Gamble, 3-M, Siemens in Germany, or Hitachi in Japan, do consistently so much better in the introduction and development of their products than most others. One reason is that businesses with a high batting average tend to appraise their innovation performance against expectations. Most businesses manage innovation by promise; the competent innovators manage by feedback from results.

4. *Strategies versus performance*: Finally, the performance of management can and should be measured against its business strategies. Did the things that the strategy expected to happen in fact take place? And were the goals set the right goals, in light of actual development, both within the business and in the market, economy, and society? And have they been attained? To judge strategies against performance requires that expectations be defined and spelled out, and that there be organized feedback from actual events on the expectations. As with innovation, the most capable firm does not have a particularly high batting average in its business strategies, something less than 0.300 I would assume. But, to continue the baseball metaphor, these managements at least know when they strike out or make a hit. Above all, they know what they do well and what they need to improve on.

3

Managing the Sea-Change: The New Population Structure and the New Population Dynamics

Managing the Sea-Change: The New Population Structure and the New Population Dynamics

None of the headline-makers with which we are so constantly bombarded—neither OPEC nor all the promised shortages of food, metals, or minerals that are now so widely predicted, nor any other "crisis" of the moment—are nearly as important, let alone as real, as the changes taking place in population structure and population dynamics. Yet few businesses, and fewer governments, have even perceived them. The most important change is not the much discussed "population explosion" in the developing countries, massive though that is. The truly important and yet unperceived development ahead is the imminent labor shortage in the developed countries, and especially the shortage of young people available for traditional jobs in manufacturing and services. All developed countries, including those of the Communist bloc—that is, the European parts of the Soviet Union and Russia's European satellites—face drastic shifts in the size, the age structure, the educational structure, and the composition of their labor force—a result in part of the "baby boom" in the non-Communist countries from the late forties until the mid-sixties, and even more of the "baby bust" that began in the developed Communist countries during and after World War II and reached all developed countries by the late sixties.

Population dynamics will create new opportunities: new markets and new patterns of economic integration. They will create the need for new policies, especially social policies such as the need to anticipate and to provide for structural redundancies in the developed countries. Both the West's approach through unemployment benefits and Japan's policy of "lifetime employment" are at best partial successes and quite inadequate. Above all, population dynamics will stand on their head some of the most cherished beliefs and habits of business and government, of employers, trade unions, and employees. They will challenge the accepted concepts of international economics and international trade by largely replacing international trade in finished goods with "production sharing." They will challenge widely held beliefs regarding the structure and segmentation of consumer markets. They are likely to transform the traditional "multinational corporation" into a "multinational confederation." They will create labor shortages and labor surpluses simultaneously, confounding traditional concepts and measurements of employment and unemployment. They will force the developed countries to make employment opportunities for the highly educated in managerial and professional jobs the overriding priority, while at the same time creating pressures to protect the jobs of unskilled or semiskilled people at the risk of economic impoverishment. They will make obsolete a cherished achievement of the last hundred years: "retirement" at a fixed age. They will altogether transform the labor force in the developed countries—to the point where there is no more "traditional" labor force, to the point indeed where there is not one "labor force" but only "labor forces," each with its own different needs, expectations, and performance characteristics.

Population dynamics are rapidly transforming traditional organization into a "double-headed monster" in which autonomous managerial and autonomous professional organizations live together in symbiotic tension. These dynamics create the need for new and different economic, social, and organizational strategies.

The New Realities

In the twenty-first century, population structure and population dynamics may well again be stable, if not static. But in the last decades of the twentieth century, population structures will be the least stable and most drastically changing element in economics, society, and world politics, and probably the single most important cause of turbulence.

Economists, businessmen, and politicians have always known that population matters. But they usually paid no further attention—and were usually justified in so doing. For population shifts tended to occur on a time scale that made them irrelevant to the decisions businessmen or politicians have to make, decisions that have a time span of five to ten years, as against the forty or fifty years of traditional population changes.

But during the second half of the twentieth century, the time span of population changes mutated. Population changes now are occurring within exceedingly short time periods. And population changes have become radical, erratic, contradictory—yet more predictable than anything else. Anyone in the labor force of the developed countries by the year 2000 is already born. But so too are most of the people in the labor force of the developing countries, even though the age of entrance into work is so much lower there than in the developed world (still only fourteen or fifteen, as it was in the developed world before World War II).

In all developed countries of the free world there was a "baby boom" after World War II. It started in the United States, where the number of live births increased by almost 50 percent within the two years 1947–49—a totally unprecedented jump, and one for which we have no explanation. Japan followed suit in the early fifties with an equal, if not greater, increase in birth numbers. The last major developed country in the free world to have a "baby boom" was Germany. There the boom began in the mid-fifties.

But then one developed country of the free world after the other had an equally unprecedented "baby bust." It started first in Japan, in the late fifties, hit the United States in 1960, and finally reached Germany by the late 1960s. In every single developed country (except Great Britain only, where there was not much of a "baby boom" to correct) the number of live births went down by an unprecedented 25 to 30 percent. It has stayed at the bottom since then.

The only difference between the developed countries of the free world and the developed countries of the Communist bloc (European Russia and Russia's European satellites) is that the developed Soviet bloc countries had no "baby boom" at all. European Russia did not even make up the tremendous losses in babies and children during World War II, when for four or five years practically no babies were born—and those that were born did not survive—and when an extraordinary proportion of children perished. In the Communist satellites of central Europe, World War II produced no such ravages. But there was also no "baby boom" after the war. In all developed Communist countries, birthrates are at an unprecedented low. European Russia probably has the lowest birthrate recorded in peacetime for any country except in the last stages of social and political disintegration. (In the Roman Empire during the barbarian invasions the birthrate, or rather the rate of surviving children, was probably as low as in European Russia today, though probably no lower.) And Czechoslovakia, Hungary, Poland, Bulgaria, and Rumania have birthrates that are equally low—well below the net reproduction requirements.

In all developed countries, except again Great Britain, the postwar years brought an unprecedented educational shift that has changed drastically the age of entrance into the labor force and the expectations of the young people entering upon work and careers. Most extreme, as in all other demographic events, was Japan. Before World War II, only three or four out of every twenty young Japanese went to high school. The other sixteen or seventeen finished their formal education with junior high school. Now half of the young male Japanese attend university. The other half goes to work after finishing high school. Young men who still go to work when they have finished junior high are all but unknown today; and young women who stop their schooling at age fifteen, with junior high school, can be found only in a few remote rural areas.

In all developed countries, life expectancies have risen dramatically. When the United States introduced governmental pensions in the Social Security legislation of 1935, the actuaries counted on a median life expectancy of fifty-eight years for men. It is now well over seventy and rising. The people who, forty-five years ago, survived to age sixty-five had a life expectancy of a few months only. Today the sixty-five-year-old man or woman can expect to live another thirteen to fourteen years. And most people who reach age sixty-five in the developed countries today are physically and mentally "middle-aged," and able to function normally.

The most extreme case is again Japan. Before World War II, the Japanese life expectancy at birth was forty-eight years for men and fifty-two for women. These figures did not change until 1950. Now, thirty years later, Japan has the highest life expectancies of any country in the world—well into the seventies for both sexes.

There is practically no difference between the developed market-economy countries and the developed Communist countries so far as the educational shift and the lengthening of life and working-life span are concerned. In all of them a much larger proportion of the young stay in school five to seven years longer than they did fifty years ago. In all of them the most rapidly growing segment of the population has been and will be the older age group.

In Japan, people sixty-five years and older constituted only 7 percent of the population—one out of every fifteen—in 1970; by 1990, the figure will have risen to 14 percent—one out of every seven Japanese and one out of every four adults. Sweden will have about the same proportion of older people, and they may be a larger proportion of the adult population. In the United States, the over-sixty-five-year-olds will constitute, by 1990, one-eighth of the total population and at least one-sixth of the adults. People aged over fifty-five—the age when people first begin to be conscious of retirement and of the need to provide for their old age—will constitute a majority or near-majority of the adult population in every developed country by the year 2000.

During the postwar period, the composition of the labor force changed dramatically. When the United States first developed official unemployment statistics in 1935, it was assumed without discussion or argument that "employed" meant a male adult head of household supporting a family and working full time. Of course many women worked in 1935. But except for those who were not paid and thus not counted at all, such as farmers' wives or the wives of small shopkeepers, they were either domestic servants, now all but extinct, or young unmarried women who were expected to find a husband, start a family, and leave the work force for good.

Male adult heads of household still account in 1980 for seven out of every ten hours worked in America. But they have become a distinct minority in numbers and no more than two-fifths of the people at work in the country today. Three-fifths, a clear majority, are people who forty-five years ago were hardly considered and rarely even counted: women who will stay permanently in the labor force, at least as part-time workers; older people past retirement age, working either full time or part time; students in school or college—white, black, and Mexican—available mainly for part-time work; and so on.

American employment and unemployment statistics still assume that everybody at work works full time and that every "unemployed" is available for full-time permanent work. They still assume that the "unemployed" is ipso facto male, adult, and the head of a household who supports other people. Yet these assumptions are absurd by now—for every developed country.

The labor force has become heterogeneous; and its fragmentation will continue. Such splintering will continue in respect to age and sex distribution—even in Japan, women increasingly either stay in the labor force after marriage or return to it (full time or part time) after their children are past infancy. Fragmentation will continue in respect to full-time and part-time work. The majority of hours are likely to be still worked by adult male heads of household who consider themselves full-time employes and look for a steady job. But in numbers other employes will predominate everywhere in developed countries—women, for instance, married or unmarried. Many (a majority among the younger ones) will be working full time and will expect the same opportunities as men. But many, perhaps the majority of both older and younger women, will expect different benefits. What appears as a "benefit" or as an "opportunity" to the traditional male employe often has little appeal to the working woman, for example, a company retirement plan when the woman is married to a man who already has an equally good or better retirement plan at his place at work; health-care benefits when the woman's husband has health insurance for the family at his place of business; or advancement through a transfer to another location when the working woman is tied to her family and has a husband with a job of his own.

Increasingly, also, there will be people who look upon their job as a place to practice their special skill, and especially highly technical skills, and who look upon their employer—whether university, hospital, or business—as a "facility." Their "loyalty" and "allegiance" will be to their craft, their tools, their discipline, their methodology, rather than to a company, a university, a community. Increasingly, we will employ people who resemble the itinerant journeyman of yesterday and who work full time for one employer and for one period, then part time for another employer and another period.

Equally important will be the change in what "age" means. Before the nineteenth century, there was no "retirement age" and no "pension plan"—people were expected to die young. When a "retirement age" was first established (Bismarck's Germany in the 1880s pioneered the concept), people were not expected to survive to it and certainly not expected to reach it in good health and able to work. Traditional pension systems—their remnants are still around us—were designed to take care of surviving widows and minor children rather than to provide the superannuated employe with a retirement pension.

The system that still prevails in most Japanese companies, especially the smaller ones, was designed only fifty years ago, in the twenties. The employe retires at age fifty-five with a separation payment equal to two or three years of salary. But if an employe dies before reaching age fifty-five, his surviving widow and minor children are looked after reasonably well. Fifty years ago when Japanese life expectancies were in the forties, this was not an unreasonable system. Now, when the fifty-five-year-old Japanese can expect to live another twenty years or longer, it is totally inappropriate.

But, of course, the fifty-five-year-old Japanese does not "retire"; he cannot afford it. He keeps on working, with another employer, usually a small company and at a much lower salary, or "self-employed" as a craftsman or casual worker. The same pattern can now be found in all developed countries. It is still widely assumed that the man or woman who "retires" stops working, but this is more and more an exception rather than the rule. An ever-larger proportion, especially in these inflationary times, keep on working, though usually for a different employer, or part time, or on casual jobs. And in increasing numbers these non-retired retirees do not report their earnings to an increasingly rapacious tax collector.

In the Soviet Union there is virtually no income tax. All the taxes, and they are exorbitantly high, are taxes on consumption hidden in the price of consumer goods. There is therefore no incentive to keep secret one's income after retirement. So we know that in Russia practically all retired employes under seventy or seventy-five work full time or part time; if they didn't, the Soviet economy would collapse. But even in the developed non-Communist countries, where retirement pensions are much more generous than in the parsimonious Soviet Union, a majority of the people who are officially reported as "retired" and as having no income except their (usually tax-free) retirement pensions are almost certainly working, at least part time.

The only choice developed countries have is either to accept that traditional retirement ages have ceased to make sense—as the United States is in the process of doing—or to pretend that there is official, mandatory retirement at a certain age and then close both eyes to the fact that "retired" people continue to work and not report their incomes, as is increasingly the case in western Europe. European trade union demands for a lower "mandatory" retirement age can only make this hypocrisy more prevalent. Traditional "mandatory" retirement at any fixed age is dead, partly because the people reaching this traditional age cannot stand being idle while still in good physical and mental shape, and partly because the economy cannot support them in idleness once the over-sixty-fives in every developed country make up one-fifth or one-fourth of the adult population.

But equally important is the change at the other end, the age of entrance. There is very little evidence that jobs have become more demanding. In English-speaking Canada, for example, banks have recruited college graduates for entrance positions for the last twenty years, and now tend to demand an additional master of business administration degree. But in French-speaking Quebec, where the education revolution came quite a bit later, the same Canadian banks hire high school graduates for entrance positions—and these French-Canadians are no less productive, no less prepared, no less equal to the demands of the job than their English-speaking colleagues to the west who have sat in school for an additional four to six years.

The foreman in the Detroit automobile assembly plant in 1929 had, on average, two years of grade school. Yet he had a more demanding job, a bigger job, and a far more independent job than the college graduate who is foreman in 1980 and who is hedged in by a union contract, a Personnel Department, quality control, production scheduling, a training supervisor, and so on—none of which the 1929 foreman had ever heard about.

The main reason for demanding higher education for entrance to jobs may be the very real and growing need to postpone going to work now that people can be expected to stay on working so much longer. But whatever the reason, the entrance age into the labor force has changed to the point where, in developed countries (except again the United Kingdom), anybody who fails to go on into advanced education is in danger of being considered a "dropout" who will never amount to much. Qualitatively, this means that the largest single group of young people entering the labor force—and certainly a majority of young men—now enter with expectations that traditional manual jobs cannot satisfy. They expect a career rather than a job. They expect to work as skilled people, and to hold managerial or professional, or at least technical, jobs. They are not prepared or qualified, whether technically or mentally, for the traditional jobs of yesterday—for the jobs on the farm, in the factory, in the mine, or for any kind of manual work, skilled or unskilled.

To sum up: the labor force of 1940, at the eve of World War II, consisted primarily of male workers, working with their hands in the factory or in the farm. The labor force of the 1980s is bisexual. In all developed countries, the proportion of women in the work force, and especially of women under fifty, is equal to the proportion of men, though a good many of the women work part time only. It is, secondly, a labor force in which an increasing number of the young people have had an advanced education and are simply not available for the traditional jobs, almost irrespective of pay. It is a labor force that is heterogeneous: it consists of men working full time and heading a family, but also increasingly of women working full time and of women (divorced ones, mainly) heading a family. Increasingly, it contains part-timers: women; young people still at school or not yet ready to start a career, let alone a family; old people who are officially past retirement age, available for full-time work for a few months or for part-time work only; and so on.

In all the developed countries the supply of young people entering into the labor force and available for traditional jobs will be exceedingly tight. We face a major shortage of traditional workers for traditional jobs, and especially for traditional manufacturing jobs.

This will not be apparent in the developed countries of the West for a few more years, because the last cohorts of the baby boom are still coming in. But the young people who will graduate from American colleges in June of 1980 are the babies of 1959, the last full year of the baby boom. After that, the number of young people available for entrance positions is going to fall fast—although the number of young people with advanced degrees beyond the bachelor's degree will still stay high for a few more years in the United States. In Germany, which started the baby boom last and ended it last, there will be a substantial supply of young people through the year 1984—but not beyond. After that, there will be no country in the developed world in which the supply of young people, and especially of young people available for traditional jobs, will not be severely restricted, and well below anything the developed countries have ever experienced. In Japan, the country that had the earliest "baby bust," this has already happened.

Most severe will be the situation in the developed countries of the Communist world, in European Russia and her European satellites. In those countries there are no baby boom cohorts to alleviate the shortage. The participation of women in the labor force is already exceedingly high. There also, retired people are already working—at least part time—if only because retirement pensions are low. And the only available labor supply is locked up in the world's least productive farming system, the collective farm that Stalin imposed on Russia just at the time when it had become technologically and economically the wrong agricultural system.

The developing countries face almost the opposite of the population configuration of the developed world. To be sure, life expectancies have gone up in these countries too, so that there will be more older people. But the important population development in the developing countries after World War II was the drastic drop in infant mortality. Of every ten babies born in Mexico in 1938, only two or three were alive and capable of work twenty years later. Of every ten babies born in Mexico in 1958, twenty years later, in 1978, seven or eight were alive and capable of work. Mexico is typical of the developing world: of Southeast Asia and of Africa, of Latin America and of the Asian parts of the Soviet Union. It is not that birthrates increased—this widely held belief is a misunderstanding. Birthrates actually have declined everywhere. But survival rates have gone up faster than birthrates have fallen.

The Mexican birthrate per thousand women of childbearing age today is significantly below what it was in 1938. But the fact that three to four times as many Mexican babies survive into adulthood means a tremendous growth in population and in the number of young people.

The growth did not start until 1960. When the experts designed the "Alliance for Progress" for Latin America in the first year of John Kennedy's presidency, they did not yet foresee any change in population dynamics. They assumed a drop in infant mortality, but a modest and slow one. Instead, during the next five years, from 1960 to 1965, infant mortality in Latin America went down very sharply and the number of young people who survived skyrocketed.

These young people are now, in the early 1980s, reaching adulthood. Through the rest of the century the basic problem of the developing world will therefore be jobs. Food should be available if only the jobs are there.

By the year 2010 or so, population can be expected to be in rough balance again in most developing countries. A balance has already been reached in the non-Communist countries of Hong Kong, Taiwan, and Singapore, and in South Korea, which is very much Chinese in its culture and traditions. Even in Latin America, most countries are moving toward population balance and sharply slower growth. And in "socialist" countries—in Indochina after the Communist takeover and in the socialist countries of Africa—politically induced mass starvation is already changing survival rates, especially the survival rates of babies and infants, few of whom can have survived the last few years in South Vietnam, in Cambodia, or in Uganda.

But between now and the year 2010, for the next thirty years, the central factor in most developing countries will be the aftermath of their tremendous success in keeping babies alive. The drop in infant mortality in the thirty years after World War II is one of mankind's success stories. The consequences have yet to be faced.

The Unique Russian Dilemma

In this world of population changes the position of the Soviet Union is unique, for it is at once a developed country in its European parts and a developing one in Soviet Asia. The radically opposed population dynamics of these two parts may put Russia's very survival through the rest of this century in serious doubt.

Russia is the one surviving nineteenth-century empire. It is the only nation that contains within its boundaries the demographics of the developed world and of the developing world, both in an extreme form. European Russia has the lowest birthrate of all countries today. It had no "baby boom" and therefore, unlike the countries of the West, no large labor supply of young adults. It has undergone very much the same educational shift as the West. And as in the West, life expectations have been moving inexorably upward. Of all societies today, European Russia is thus by far the oldest. Mr. Brezhnev at age seventy-three or seventy-four is considered an old man—and in terms of physical and apparently also mental health, he is indeed elderly. But the Russian problem is precisely the lack of younger people to succeed his generation. Any visitor to Russia comments on the absence of vigorous, early-middle-aged people in all areas.

At the same time, European Russia faces singularly difficult problems in tapping its one and only labor reservoir: the unproductive people on the farm. The collective farm has become a welfare institution. The able, competent, and ambitious ones left long ago and are in the cities. What is left behind are unproductive people, inhibited by the system from becoming productive, but with a guaranteed low income as long as they stay on the farm. To abolish the collective farm altogether and switch to large family farms producing for the market—the only truly efficient form of agriculture in Russia under modern technological conditions—is politically impossible and would require an overthrow of the regime. And educated Russians are as unwilling to do manual work as educated people anywhere else.

The Russians, anticipating their population squeeze as early as 1970, attempted an extreme policy change. Since the mid-twenties, when Stalin took over, foreign capital had been shut out of Russia, as much because of the fear of the foreign manager and technician and the ideological contamination he would bring as because of nationalist pride. But since 1970 the Soviet Union has pushed the importation of entire capital-goods plants, all of them highly automated and in partnership with large companies from the "capitalist world," such as Fiat: plants to produce automobiles, trucks, heavy machine tools, or ships. To do this, the Soviet Union and its satellites went heavily into debt to the "capitalist" world, beyond the point at which debt service can be taken for granted—something the Soviet Union had always avoided as a major sin against the basic Marxist creed, and as certain to corrupt.

This attempt to prevent the consequences of demographics has, however, been an unqualified failure. Even if some plants will eventually come on stream—and so far, most of them are still projects only, despite enormous capital investment—they will be labor-intensive rather than auto-mated. In fact, the very kind of labor these plants will require, namely, skilled maintenance workers, foremen, and technicians, are the people in shortest supply in the Soviet Union.

This leaves only one alternative within the traditional structure of Soviet society: a sharp scaling down of the military.

At the same time, the population of the Asian parts of the Soviet Union is rapidly expanding, especially in numbers of young people. Non-European, Asian people are already a majority in the Soviet Union. By the year 2000, two-thirds of the population of the present area of the Soviet Union will be Asiatics, with about half of them Moslem. Yet so far the Asian people in the Soviet Union have not been admitted to any position of power and prestige. The great majority, perhaps three-quarters, do not speak Russian; yet all business in the Soviet Union is carried on in Russian. Very few, if any, important positions in government, in the Communist Party, in the university, and in industry are held by Asiatics. Nor are they represented in science, in technology, or in the arts. Above all, so far there are few officers of Asian origin in command positions in the Russian armed services, which are as strictly reserved for white Europeans as they were under the czar.

As a result of demographics, the Soviet Union thus faces internal problems for which communism has no answers. It will have to retrench either industrially or militarily, or it will have to reform the collective farm, which can hardly be done without political convulsion. It cannot escape rising tensions between the population of a developed European Russia and the fast-growing populations of a developing Asian Russia. Within the next twenty-five years the Soviet Union will be faced by the same kind of racial, ethnic, religious, and cultural tensions that have split asunder all other nineteenth-century empires since World War II.

The next few years may thus be the most dangerous years in

world politics since the end of World War II. They are the last years in which a hardliner in the Kremlin can expect to gain military and political supremacy on the basis of Russia's traditional policy. After that, the manpower advantage will rapidly shift against the Soviet Union, unless indeed the Soviet Union imposes on itself the high-risk experiment of letting its military forces become primarily Asian—with command positions in the hands of Asians. To some extent relief can be provided by hiring mercenaries, a policy the Soviet Union is already following in using the Cubans in Africa and in allowing its client-state, Vietnam, to conduct what is in effect war against China and the Chinese. But the temptation to use these next few years to tilt the balance of power once and for all against the West must be great, whether this means (as western Europeans fear) attack across the Elbe or, perhaps more likely, outflanking western Europe through military or ideological occupation of the petroleum-producing areas of the Middle East.

The End of the Migrations

The Western developed countries which also face a sharp drop in the traditional labor force can no longer expect to compensate for it by bringing in new immigrants from developing pre-industrial areas. The post-World War II period solved its own comparatively minor population problems through mass migrations. This solution will no longer be available in most parts of the world.

The quarter century between the Marshall Plan and the petroleum crisis was a period of worldwide migrations. People in very large numbers moved from pre-industrial into industrial and urban environments. In some areas—the United States, Japan, the Soviet Union—these mass migrations occurred within a national economy.

Japan at the end of World War II still had three-fifths of her people in rural areas, with the majority of them working the land; today, rural Japan accounts for less than a fifth of the total population, and farmers for only 10 percent. In the United States, similarly, the rural population has fallen by two-thirds since World War II—people who make their living as farmers now account for fewer than one in twenty of America's families. In the Soviet Union, one-quarter of the population is still locked up in low-productivity farms—but in 1945 the proportion was almost 50 percent.

In western Europe there were similar movements from the farm, especially in southern Germany, Italy, Spain, and Greece. But the main migration in western Europe was from the pre-industrial parts of Europe, that is the South, the Mediterranean, Spain, Sicily, Greece, Portugal, Turkey, Algeria, Yugoslavia, to the industrial West and North. In some countries, for example Switzerland, "guest workers" outnumbered native workers in many industries by the end of the sixties.

There is only one country left where a migration will still continue: the United States. America can expect large-scale migration from Mexico, a very poor country with one of the largest labor surpluses and one of the highest unemployment rates, yet located next to the richest country and one of its richest areas, the Southwest, with a very low supply of indigenous young people for traditional jobs.

There is no way to prevent mass migration from Mexico over an open 2,000-mile border into the United States, both into the Southwest from San Diego to Denver and into the metropolitan areas of the East and Midwest—New York, Philadelphia, and Chicago—with their already large Hispanic populations. Indeed, the *reconquista* of southern California by Mexican immigrants has already begun. By the year 2000, Hispanic-Americans should account for some 50 million of an American population of 250 million; they are about 15 million now. Whether they are officially "legal," "illegal," or "quasi-legal" is immaterial. In any event, the Southwest of the United States may be the only region in the developed world to show a sizable growth in traditional manufacturing industry over the next twenty or twenty-five years.

Socially and culturally, a mass migration of Mexicans to the United States will exacerbate racial and ethnic tensions. With a near-majority in America becoming Roman Catholics in a country of the "Protestant ethos," religion might become a political issue again. There might even be a "black backlash" as the "Chicanos" from Mexico threaten to displace the American black as the officially "disadvantaged" and thus officially privileged "minority." But these are exactly the problems the United States is used to and has handled—or mishandled—throughout all her history. Economically, the mass migration from Mexico, whatever the labor unions might say, should be beneficial and should in fact endow American manufacturing with competitive strength such as it has not known for quite some time.

But in the rest of the developed Western world migration will not provide relief. The reservoirs of underemployed workers that fed the American and Japanese industrial econ-omies in the post-World War II period are largely drained. There are few pre-industrial people left on the American and Japanese farm; the "small" farmers in these two countries mainly work in industry already, though they live on a marginal farm and raise a few chickens. Immigration of non-Japanese, Vietnamese, for instance, into Japan is almost unthinkable—the Japanese have not yet absorbed the handful of Koreans who came in many years ago. As for western Europe, further mass immigration of "guest workers" is quite unlikely. These societies will not accept any more of the turbulence that the immigrations of the last twenty-five years have produced. One way or another, every one of the devel-oped societies of western Europe will do what the Swiss and

Germans are doing already, cut back on immigrants and "guest workers" rather than encourage further migration from pre-industrial into industrial areas.

We have known for more than 250 years, ever since the father of statistics, Sir William Petty, first looked at the burgeoning cities of the early eighteenth century in the Lancashire and Yorkshire of his time, that there are limits to the absorptive capacity of an urban civilization. If the stream of migrants becomes too great, social turbulence sets in. In that respect, the black ghettos of today's large American cities do not look too different from the horrible slums in which, in my childhood, the Czechs had settled when they moved to Vienna around 1900. The Liverpool or Manchester of 1850 that Friedrich Engels knew was quite similar to the world today's novelist describes when he writes of the Turin of the Sicilians in northern Italy, of the barrios of the "Chicano" in east Los Angeles, or of the slums of the Turkish "guest workers" in the German Ruhr. Equally contemporaneous is the world Charles Dickens described in his frightening novel *Hard Times*, written in the early 1840s, about the Lancashire of the cotton mills, with their despairing brutalized proletarians who were totally lost in the industrial jungle.

Further mass migrations will clearly be frowned upon and kept to a minimum. The developed world, by and large, will therefore have to make do with the labor force it has. It will have to accept a sharp drop in the number of young people reaching working age; a sharp upgrading of schooling, and with it of expectations on the part of young people; an increasing heterogeneity of the labor force—women equalling men in their participation but not necessarily in their concept of what a "job" is; "work" no longer necessarily meaning a full-time lifetime job; and the end of mandatory retirement age and, especially, of the assumption that the person who "retires" automatically stops "working."

In the developing countries, on the other hand, the over-riding problem economically, socially, and politically will be to find jobs for a veritable tide of young people reaching working age—young people who are not very highly trained or very highly skilled but who are more highly trained and skilled than their parents were, have a much wider horizon if only because of radio and television, who know how the rich world lives; young people, above all, who no longer live in remote mountain valleys but in large and fast-growing urban centers and who therefore are visible and can make themselves seen and heard.

These are the realities.

Production Sharing: The Transnational Integration

In the developed countries the costs of traditional work, especially traditional manufacturing work, must rise because of the labor shortage. But even sharply higher wages for traditional work will not procure the labor needed to do the work; the people simply will not be available. The capacity of the developed countries to produce must go down unless they can obtain elsewhere a labor force for the labor-intensive stages of production.

The developing countries in turn face a decline in their economic position and national product—apart from severe threats to their social and political stability—unless they can find work for their surplus labor, labor that is qualified only for traditional labor-intensive work. They have neither the technology, the capital, nor the management to develop their own integrated industries; nor, in most cases, do they have the markets to generate the demand for the products such industries would turn out. For those stages of production that require technology and high management skills, they will increasingly have to depend on the developed world and its surplus of trained and educated people. And only in the developed world can developing countries hope to find adequate markets for the products of their surplus labor.

The practice of production sharing will therefore be the most important form of economic integration, needed by developed and developing countries alike. In production sharing the resources of the developing countries—their abundant labor for traditional jobs—are brought together with the resources of the developed countries—their management, their technology, their educated people, their markets and purchasing power.

Men's shoes sold in the United States usually start out as the hide on an American cow. As a rule, however, the hide is not tanned in the United States but shipped to a place like Brazil for tanning. Tanning is highly labor-intensive work, for which not enough workers are available in America. The leather is then shipped—perhaps through the intermediary of a Japanese trading company—to the Caribbean. Part of it may be worked up into uppers in the British Virgin Islands, part into soles in Haiti. Then uppers and soles are shipped to islands like Barbados or Jamaica, the products of which have access to Britain and to the European Common Market, and to Puerto Rico, where they are worked up into shoes that enter the United States under the American tariff umbrella.

What are these shoes by origin? The hide, though the largest single cost element, still constitutes no more than one-quarter of the manufacturer's cost for the shoe. By labor content, these are "imported shoes"; by skill content, they are "American-made." Surely these are truly transnational shoes. Anything that has a heavy labor content is processed in developing countries. The raising of the cow, which is a most capital-intensive process, heavily automated, and requiring the greatest skill and advanced management, is done in a developed country that has necessary skills, knowledge, and equipment. The management of the entire process—the design of the shoes, their quality control, and their marketing—is also done entirely in developed countries, where the manpower and the skills needed for these tasks are available.

Another example of production sharing is the hand-held electronic calculator. It may carry the nameplate of a Japanese company but this is the only thing on it that is "Made in Japan." The electronic chips came from the United States, either from Dallas or from "Silicone Valley," outside San Francisco. They were assembled in Singapore, in Malaya, in Indonesia, perhaps in Nigeria—wherever a Chinese subcontractor was available. The steel for the housing may be the product of an Indian steel mill built originally to produce steel for an Indian automotive industry that never came into being. And then, in some free-port zone in Kobe or Yokohama, the label "Made in Japan" was put on. The calculator is sold all over the world, with the bulk, of course, in developed countries. The design, the quality control, and the marketing were done by a Japanese company located in a highly developed country. The stages of production that require high technology, tight quality control, high capital investment— the design and manufacture of the chips—were also done in a developed country, the United States. But the labor-intensive work was done in developing countries.

The examples could be multiplied ad infinitum, for production sharing has been the fastest-growing segment of international trade these last ten years. Production sharing—a term I coined a few years ago and still not in wide use—is increasingly becoming the dominant mode of economic integration throughout the non-Communist world.

Production sharing makes very high demands on design, marketing, and quality control, and even higher ones on the management skills of planning, organizing, integrating, and coordinating. But it renders secondary, if not unimportant, capital investment, which is the traditional means of control and integration. It requires no more than a minimum of capital investment in the developing country. If the subcontractor in Morocco, Nigeria, or Malaya has a firm order in his hand from a major marketing company in the developed world, he can finance himself through conventional short-term bank credit.

A well-known electronics company, one of the pioneers of semiconductor technology, has more than 12,000 people—half its labor force—in West Africa and does two-thirds of its manufacturing work there. But when I asked how much company capital was invested in West Africa, the answer was: "Two Pan-American round-trip tickets a month." All the rest is bank credit obtained by the West African subcontractor against the parent company's firm commitment to buy the products of West African labor.

A second, even more complex form of production sharing is pushed especially by the Japanese: the export of entire, integrated plants, which are paid for largely by their products to be marketed in the developed markets.

The Japanese are, for instance, building a huge petrochemical complex in Algeria. Algeria herself will use no more than one-tenth of the plant's output, if that much; the rest will be marketed by the Japanese builder, and sold largely in Japan. Similarly, the Japanese are building shoe-manufacturing plants in Southeast Asia, paid for by their output, which will be sold primarily in Japan.

This too is production sharing. The developed country supplies the design both of the plant and of its products; it builds the plants, indeed, exports most of it as a finished capital-intensive and technology-intensive product. And it markets the output in developed countries. Again one might ask whose "product" the petrochemicals or the shoes are. In terms of labor content they are products, of course, of the developing country; in terms of value added, they are primarily "Japanese."

Production sharing is the best hope—perhaps the only hope—for most of the developing countries to survive without catastrophe the explosive expansion of working-age people in search of a job. Neither capitalism nor communism nor any of the traditional theories of economic development has an answer to the unprecedented tripling of young people who reach working age and need jobs. The young people in the developing countries are not highly schooled or highly trained, to be sure. But they are better trained and better schooled than their parents were. More important, they are in the cities whereas yesterday's pre-industrial people were in remote and isolated rural areas. Forty years ago, when there was unrest in the countryside, the Mexican government dispatched a company of rural police. They shot and raped and spread total terror—then there was "peace and quiet" again. Nobody ever heard about the episode. The only newspapers were in the far-away capital city. Nowadays a fourteen-year-old boy in a remote pueblo hops the tailgate of a truck, and two hours later he is in a big city. Mexico has well over twenty centers, each with a population of 1 million people, whereas the Mexico of forty years ago had only Mexico City and perhaps, as a poor second, the port city of Vera Cruz. And in the city that Indian boy counts, and is both seen and heard. Every developing country has undergone a similar sea-change.

The argument being made in the developing countries against production sharing is that it is another form of colonialism and of dependence on the developed world. But practically no developing country (Brazil is probably the one exception) has the market potential today for integrated industry to provide even the minimum employment needed. Very few of them have enough of the scarcest resources—managerial, professional, entrepreneurial, and technical people—to build, organize, and run integrated industries of the needed scale. These skills cannot be improvised, nor can they be bought on the world market and imported. Only if the young people get enough jobs today—and not in the millennium—will these countries be able to develop both the "superstructure" of managerial and professional skills and the mass purchasing power they need to build up their own integrated manufacturing industries for tomorrow. In traditional terms, the availability of young people for traditional manufacturing work is the one "factor advantage" of developing countries.

To have the labor-intensive stages of production done in the developing world rather than at home represents just as much of a "dependence" for the developed countries as it does for the developing ones—interdependence is a two-way street, after all. For the standard of living of the developed world can also be maintained only if it succeeds in mobilizing the labor resources of the developing world. It has the technical resources, the entrepreneurial resources, the managerial resources—and the markets. But it lacks, and will increasingly lack, the labor resource to do the traditional stages of production.

The Need for New Theories, New Concepts, and New Measurements

Production sharing is growing rapidly, yet this growth remains largely unnoticed. So far we have no theory for it, no concepts, and no measurements. It is quite different from what is commonly called "international trade," for it represents a transnational integration that so far is barely known to the economist or government statistician.

The theory of international trade is still pretty much what it was when Adam Smith postulated it two hundred years ago. It still talks of the exchange of products between areas that have comparative advantages. Its prototype is still Adam Smith's example of the exchange of English woolens against Portuguese wines, where England's wet, cool climate encourages the production of wool and of woolen textiles and makes all but impossible the production of wine; whereas Portugal's warm, dry climate favors the production of wine and makes all but impossible the production of wool. This theory of complementary trade is still essentially what international economists teach and write about.

But since 1880 or so, for an entire century, the reality of international trade has become quite different. It has meant the exchange of competitive products, the exchange of the machine tools of one country against the machine tools of another country. It is typified by the trade pattern of the chemical industry. Every single chemical company has other chemical companies as both the largest customers and the most serious competitors. And Switzerland, with 5 million people or so, is a far better customer for American manufactured products than all of India, with one hundred times the population. For the more a country industrializes, the more do its customers become other industrialized countries.

We are about to enter the stage of integrated trade, for this is what production sharing means. Yet economists, theoreticians, and policymakers are totally unprepared for the challenge. In fact, the lack of concepts and of measurements is a serious problem. Our concepts cannot as yet handle production sharing.

A government statistician will record the export of hides from America as "exports" and the import of shoes as "imports"; his figures will nowhere relate the two. The American cattle grower does not even know that his livelihood depends on the sale of foreign-made shoes in the American market, for hides represent the margin between breaking even and making a profit for the livestock grower in Nebraska. Nor, conversely, does the Haitian manufacturer of the soles for these American shoes realize that he depends on hides grown in the United States. No one yet perceives the relationships. And when shoe workers' unions in the United States or shoe manufacturers in North Carolina agitate for a ban on the importation of "cheap foreign imports," no cattle grower in the Great Plains realizes that they are actually agitating to ban the export of American hides on which his livelihood depends. When the American tanning industry—as it does—asks for a ban on sending hides abroad, American shoe retailers (let alone American consumers) do not realize that this would mean having no shoes to sell in American shops. They do not know that there are not enough American workers available to do even a fraction of the tanning needed.

Production sharing defies traditional concepts, of foreign trade, of national economies, and of products altogether. And yet it is becoming the only available form of economic integration, the only form in which the resources of developed, as well as of developing, countries can productively be used for their mutual benefit. Very few countries see this so far, though some of the developing countries such as the non-Communist Chinese are well ahead of the developed ones in this respect. It is not only that governments will resist the trend; it defies all their notions of what is "proper." Labor unions will resist it even more.

One of the most successful examples of production sharing in the automotive industry, the Ford Fiesta, will no longer be sold in the United States because of governmental and union resistance, even though the Fiesta has superior gasoline consumption and a low pollution level. The concept of the Fiesta was American, as were the specifications. The actual design was then done in Germany. Germany produced the engine and frame; Mexico the transmission and the brakes; Canada the electrical system. It was finally assembled in the United States for the American market. The Fiesta became a highly successful car of that market; but the unions succeeded in making sure that it will not be sold in the United States, despite its success and despite the fact that it gives employment to American assembly labor. The unions got the American energy agencies to rule that only cars that are totally "American" in their labor content will be counted among the cars the American-based automobile manufacturer can sell under the energy-saving requirements. If the Fiesta were made by a totally non-American company, it could be imported. Being made by "production sharing" under an American nameplate, it is an offense to labor unions, an enigma to bureaucrats, and taboo to both.

From Multinational Corporation to Transnational Confederation

The emergence of production sharing as the prevailing form of worldwide economic integration in the years ahead means that the future is unlikely to be with the old "multinationals." But it is also unlikely to take the shape that the critics of the multinationals, especially in the developing countries, thought it would. There is a great deal of talk about "multinationals" today, yet there really is no such animal. What we have had, in the twenty-five years since the Marshall Plan, is a resurgence of the nineteenth-century pattern of economic integration, in which a company in a developed country has subsidiaries and affiliates abroad, with the center of gravity remaining where the original headquarters are. The traditional nineteenth-century "international company" was a national company with subsidiaries, affiliates, and branches abroad—and so is today's "multinational."

Actually, a larger share of manufacturing was "multinational" before World War I than it is today. And in the world before 1914, no one thought that such "multinational" companies were anything extraordinary. Fiat in Italy, for instance, was founded in Turin on New Year's Day 1900. By 1903 or 1905, Austro-Fiat, the wholly owned Austrian subsidiary, was quite a bit larger than the parent company, for the old Austro-Hungarian Empire was a far bigger and more developed market than the Italy of 1900. Austro-Fiats, which were cars designed in Turin but made in Vienna, were even adopted as the staff cars for the Austro-Hungarian Army—and no one in those days thought this odd. Similarly, Siemens, founded in Germany around 1856, was by the 1860s larger in Great Britain and in Russia than in its original German markets. Great Britain was the most highly developed country of Europe and of the world, so that British Siemens had a much bigger market than the parent company, which, until 1880 or so, was still operating in a developing country. And Russia between 1860 and 1880 had a boom in railway construction that made Siemens, then the foremost European supplier of telegraph equipment, a monopoly supplier. Three months after Edison had demonstrated his first, still very primitive, incandescent light bulb in New Jersey, Edison light bulbs were for sale in Great Britain and soon thereafter in Japan. A few months after Alexander Graham Bell had shown his telephone in the United States, Bell telephones were being installed in most European countries, as well as in Japan.

It was taken for granted in the last half of the nineteenth century and up to World War I that the successful company, and especially the innovating one, would immediately become "multinational." Henry Ford, despite his xenophobia, started his English subsidiary before he began to expand his original automobile plant in Detroit.

These developments came to a halt with World War I. All that happened after World War II was that the old developments were revived. And, just as the developments before World War I had been primarily between and within developed countries, so was the development after World War II.

Raw material producers have to go where the raw materials are. If crude oil is buried beneath the sands of Saudi Arabia, raw material producers must go there. But the extractive industries are not "multinationals"; they are basically companies that produce raw materials for the markets of the developed countries. Their mines and oil fields are "suppliers" rather than "businesses." If we take the extractive industries out of the statistics, 85 percent of all the investment in "multinationals"—and especially the investment since World War II—has been by developed countries in other developed countries. This holds true for the American investment, which was primarily in Europe, especially after the start of the Common Market, and secondarily in Canada and Japan. The developing countries accounted for 5 to 8 percent of the investment. This is true even of financial institutions, though money is the least nationalistic of all economic entities. The American banks—and, following them, the British, German, Swiss, and Dutch banks—have invested primarily in other developed countries. Of the deposits of the major American multinational bank in 1979 outside the United States, 90 percent (other than OPEC money) were in and by developed countries.

Business is where the markets are. There is nothing particularly novel in this, but it is something that politicians and newspapermen tend to forget.

From now on, the "multinational" may look quite different. In the first place, it is likely to be a marketing company rather than a manufacturing company. It will be multinational because it knows how to market goods, wherever produced, in the markets of the developed countries. Secondly, it will be a management company, exercising managerial control, through technology and design. Tomorrow's multinational is likely to be a small or medium-sized company rather than a giant. Giants are too conspicuous politically. Ford could not market the Fiesta in the United States; Ford is simply too visible. The company that can organize the marketing of goods with a high transnational labor content is likely to be a company that is not a household word. To be sure, Melville, the largest American shoe retailer, with sales well above a billion dollars, is not a small company. But it is still quite invisible, especially as it markets under a number of brands (such as Thom McAn) rather than under its company name. It can thus organize a transnational production-sharing network without becoming the target for attacks by labor unions, government, or newspapers.

A medium-sized company rather than a large company has the flexibility to engage in production sharing. Such sharing requires the ability to shift fast—in design, in production, in marketing. And here the large company, which has to "plan" ten years ahead (not because the market requires it but because of its own size and complexity) is at a decided disadvantage.

The one factor the very large company can bring to bear is going to be of diminishing value, namely, the ability to provide its own capital for investment. Tomorrow's successful multinational will be based on the ability to market, rather than on the ability to invest. And there, the medium-sized company has distinct advantages.

To exploit these advantages, the multinational of tomorrow will however have to be organized quite differently from the "multinational" of today. Instead of being a "multinational corporation," it will have to become a "transnational confederation."

It will be a managing and marketing company. Above all, it will organize production and distribution. It will be organized around two focal points: technology (or design) and marketing. Insofar as it "manufactures" in its own country or in any developed country, it will concentrate on those stages of production that are least labor-intensive. The local "subsidiary" will not be a business as it has traditionally been, one that produces and markets the full range of the company's products but only in its own country. Transnational confederations will instead increasingly organize production across national boundaries and across markets, so as to optimize both labor resources and market resources. Stages of production that are labor-intensive will increasingly be done where the labor is, and increasingly not by "subsidiaries" and "branches" but by subcontractors. And the cohesion of the enterprise will come from its control of marketing rather than from its control of capital.

This will require new structures. Instead of the present pyramid, in which a central top management commands a large number of units, each of them engaged in very much the same activity, top management will act as an integrating force. Its control will be through marketing rather than through legal authority. It will lead an orchestra rather than an army. A "transnational confederation" will require both stronger top management of the entire group, and greater freedom and responsibility of the component parts. It will require what organization theory calls a "systems organization"* rather than conventional organization structures, whether functional organization or traditional decentralization. Indeed it might not be a bad idea to emulate the Japanese practice, where manufacturing and marketing in many businesses are separated and organized into two distinct companies, and to set up a separate distinct company to design and market products worldwide, while manufacturing is organized as a series of support operations.

The political dimension of the new transnationals will be even more different than the organizational one. Tradi-

---

On this, see my book *Management: Tasks, Responsibilities, Practices.*

tionally, multinationals have tried to have as little to do with the developing countries as possible. Investment in the limited and slowly growing markets of developing countries was not particularly attractive and the cost of doing business in a country like Peru or Malaya proved astronomical. Investments by multinationals in developing countries were thus not particularly profitable. Nothing is further from the truth than that a developing country was a prime target for "exploitation" on the part of manufacturing or distributive companies located in the developed country. They mainly generated losses and troubles—with but a few exceptions, such as the pharmaceutical industry. (The reason for this exception is that a poor country like Colombia cannot afford the costs of modern medical schools, modern hospitals, and modern health care. It can however afford to buy drugs that, by themselves, produce something like two-fifths of the benefits of modern medicine for about 6 to 8 percent of total costs.)

Tomorrow, the developing countries will matter to the multinationals as they have not mattered so far. They will provide the manufacturing work. The units of the transnational confederation that are based in the developing countries should increasingly become the source of goods for the business in the developed markets. The parent company should thus become increasingly dependent on them. Conversely, the transnational marketing network in the developed country should increasingly become the source of jobs for the young people in the developing countries. Transnationals will prove increasingly important to the developing countries as their channel to the markets of developed countries and as their channel to markets altogether.

Today, governments in developing countries—India and Mexico are two examples—demand capital investment by their own nationals as a condition for a foreign company to start business in their country. This simply means that the governments of poor countries insist on subsidizing companies from the rich world—the only thing this demand for participation by domestic capital can accomplish. But the demand also misses the point: the one thing to require of companies from abroad is that they create export earnings and jobs based on exports. Very few governments in the developing countries understand this as yet, except the pragmatic Chinese in Hong Kong, Taiwan, and Singapore. But some others are beginning to learn, which explains, for instance, why the Andean Pact countries on the west coast of South America again woo foreign investments.

Marketing cannot be done from a distance. It is literally impossible to sell successfully in a market that is quite different and far more advanced than the one from which the seller comes. But the developing countries will also need an influential representative with the government, the public opinion, and the labor unions of the developed countries where they have to market their labor. They will need somebody who is a part of developed society and of its political system. In other words, they will need a transnational that is accepted as a citizen of the society in which the product of their labor is to be sold. They will therefore become more dependent on the new transnational, which will surely create serious political stresses in the developing countries. It runs counter to all their rhetoric and all their deep emotions. It makes overt the fact that there is no "sovereignty" any more in an interdependent world economy.

At the same time, the relationship between the new transnational and its home country—the developed country—will also change. Traditionally, the home country has supported the multinational domiciled within its borders. It no longer does—at least as far as U.S.-based multinationals are concerned. The reason is precisely that the "multinational" is becoming a "transnational" and a symbol of worldwide economic interdependence. (On this see also Part 4 below.) Increasingly, the transnational will cut across traditional political lines and defy traditional political concepts by putting emphasis in its home country on employing skilled people rather than on creating traditional low-income low-skill jobs for manual workers; by marketing products manufactured in developing countries in exchange against design, technology, management, and marketing; and by living the reality of an integrated world economy rather than the delusion of a "national economy." Increasingly, therefore, the true political problems of the transnational confederation and of its management will lie in the developed countries, with their politicians, their labor leaders and, above all, with the inherited but hopelessly obsolete concepts and measurements of eighteenth- and nineteenth-century international economics.

The New Consumer Markets

Compared with their impact on international economy and international markets, the impacts of population structure and population dynamics on domestic markets might appear to be mild. But they are by no means insignificant. Population dynamics are causing a realignment of consumer markets in the developed countries.

Before World War I there were "markets," but there was no "market." In the United States, for instance, there were, at that time, still regional markets that had almost no contact with one another. California, and especially southern California, did not become part of the national American market until the Great Depression. But there were also sharply demarcated "class" markets. Sears, Roebuck built its business on the fact that the American farmer was a major, but separate, market; poor in terms of the individual but exceedingly potent as a mass market. And what was meant, before 1914, by "carriage trade" almost no one living today, certainly no one living in the developed countries, can imagine. For

this one has to go to India, where the 2 percent of the
population who speak English constitute a separate, more or
less affluent, market. They do not buy more of the same
goods; they buy different goods: English-language newspapers, for instance, cameras, watches, or automobiles. A
"carriage market" of this kind was a genuine and self-
contained market in every developed country before World
War I, but it no longer exists.

The West came out of World War I with "national" markets
in comparison to, say, Japan, which did not develop a national
market until after World War II. The marketing successes of
the interwar period—Sears, Roebuck and General Motors are
examples—were squarely based on the emergence of the
national market and its segmentation.

It was Alfred Sloan at General Motors who, in 1920, first
realized that America had become a national market segmented by socioeconomic income groups—from the 50 percent "low-income" group, which Sloan saw as a market for
second-hand cars, to the very small high-income group that
was to be the market for the Cadillac. Within the market for
new cars, Sloan divided the market into five categories. Each
of his five nameplates (Chevrolet, Pontiac, Oldsmobile,
Buick, and Cadillac) was positioned for a specific income
segment, but made to overlap each other so that the customer
could work his way up in the course of his economic and life
cycle. A few years later, the early quantitative approaches to
social and market analysis (e.g., the work of market and public
opinion analysts in Vienna, Austria, such as Charlotte Buehler
and Paul Felix Lazarsfeld, both of whom later came to the
United States) provided the theoretical framework and the
empirical data for what Sloan had seen intuitively as early as
1920.

By the late thirties the markets of the developed countries
were clearly segmented according to socioeconomic groups,

to the point where a trained market researcher in the United States could tell at one glance from the make and year of the automobile in the driveway and the rental value of the one-family house what a given family bought in each category and how much.

Then, in 1950, just when most everybody had accepted socioeconomic income groups as a law of nature, a new consumer market segmentation—and incidentally a new public opinion segmentation as well—appeared, superimposing itself on socioeconomic income groups: segmentation by "lifestyles."

The Edsel, designed to be the Ford Motor Company's final step in its ten-year campaign to make itself over into the image of its big competitor, General Motors, was the last automobile engineered to fit the traditional socioeconomic income segmentation. When it failed dismally, the Ford Motor Company realized, earlier than anyone else, that a fundamental shift in the consumer market was under way.

Ford's response in the form of "lifestyle cars"— Thunderbird, Mustang, and Maverick—explains in large part why the Ford Motor Company, a poor third at the end of World War II and indeed almost marginal, rapidly became a strong number two, and outside of the United States a leader among transnational automobile companies.

By the late sixties, automobile make and price had ceased to have much relationship to socioeconomic income groups and had become instead primarily a matter of division by lifestyle, at least among the groups buying new rather than second-hand cars. Car and status no longer correlated; but car and lifestyle had come to correlate very closely.

In the seventies, a new consumer segmentation has come in: segmentation by population dynamics. It will not supersede the older ones, but rather complement them. It will however create new markets.

In 1973–74, the United States underwent what everybody considered the most severe recession since the Great Depression. In terms of capital investment, it behaved like a traditional recession. Yet in terms of consumer buying, it behaved most peculiarly and in unexpected ways. "Everybody knows" that eating out is cut down sharply when there is even the slightest quaver in the economy. A restaurant meal is many times as expensive as a home-cooked meal. The only additional cost of a home-cooked meal is time—and that, in a depression, "everybody knows" is in plentiful supply. But in 1973 eating out began to boom in America. Since then it has been doubling every two years, to the point where, by 1980, every other meal eaten in the United States is an "eating-out" meal—bought in a restaurant or a fast food facility; in institutional cafeterias, in the hospital, the school, the plant, the office, and so on; or bought as a fully cooked meal, ready to be served after being taken home.

Similarly, "everybody knows" that vacation travel becomes immediately a casualty of a "recession." Yet this did not prove to be the case in 1973–74 America. Vacation travelers have indeed become exceedingly price-conscious. Minor changes in exchange rates deflect travellers from one country to another, and especially the growing majority on package tours. But the total volume of travel remained unaffected by the recession, and indeed went up sharply throughout the recession years.

"Everybody knows" that in a recession people cut back on housing. Accordingly, every American mass builder in 1973–74 rushed into what came to be known as a "basic home," essentially a home of the 1950s without the additional conveniences, appliances, and frills the intervening twenty years had added. The "basic home" did not sell at all. On the contrary, during the recession spending on housing increased.

The list could be continued indefinitely. It includes, for instance, such luxuries as sending a child to a private university at a time when, in all states of the Union, tax-supported public universities were readily available at much lower fees and were beginning in those years aggressively to campaign for students as the number of people reaching college age no longer went up. Both the highly reputed private universities and those that have a distinct character, such as fundamentalist Christian colleges, have seen the number of applicants go up, despite their high and rising fees.

Consumer markets in western Europe and in Japan have shown similar trends. This indicates that there is a new segmentation at work, a segmentation that is linked to population dynamics rather than to income. Income and perhaps even lifestyle are increasingly becoming restraints on buying rather than motivations thereof. Population segmentation is becoming the consumer market's driving force—even with inflation.

The popularity of eating out is directly related to the increasing number of married women at work, for whom time is much shorter than money. It is also related to the increased number of older people in the adult population, for whom going out to eat is often the easiest way to escape confinement and to be "in the swim."

We may thus see an increasing tendency toward markets that are sharply segmented by population dynamics. There is already a large and growing market of older people, especially of older people who live longer. And this market is recession-proof insofar as the incomes of retired people are unaffected by unemployment, mostly tax-exempt, and indexed for inflation.

Another market with fast growth in purchasing power in good times consists of young adults with high education. In this group, both sexes work (even increasingly in Japan) and both sexes therefore will have an income. In this group, however, spending patterns are different from the traditional family, in which there is one breadwinner. In the two-income family, the household budget is still tailored to the income of the male.

The young educated two-income family, in its buying behavior, does not treat the wife's income as part of the "family income." Unlike the two-income blue-collar family, it looks upon it as an extra. Household expenditure is adjusted to what the husband earns. What the wife earns is increasingly used for extraordinary—and usually major—expenses, rather than for day-to-day living.

The outstanding success in the U.S. automobile market in the years after the OPEC petroleum shock and before 1979, the Cadillac Seville, is a luxury car, selling for $15,000 to $20,000. It was designed by General Motors for the successful professional man who wants luxury, a big car with a big-car name, and yet "economy" and a slightly better fuel consumption. Until the gasoline panic of 1979, the Seville sold even better than General Motors had anticipated. But it was bought largely by women with an income of their own rather than by the professional men for whom it had been designed. The educated married working women also largely explain the increase in student applications to private fee-charging colleges. Schools that keep a record on who pays the students' bills report that the number of applicants who expect to have their college education paid for out of their mothers' earnings has gone up sharply from around one out of twenty, thirty years ago, to maybe six or eight out of twenty today.

The part-time workers probably also constitute a definite buying segment. And finally, of course, there are traditional markets: the teenagers who, though significantly fewer in numbers, will still constitute a large market even though they may no longer set fashions and determine lifestyles; and the traditional American family of father, mother, and two children, even though the mother in that family can now be expected to be at work at least part time.

Each of these markets will buy different goods. Above all, each of these markets will buy with different values. Whether one and the same marketing approach can hope to reach more than one of these groups, and in what combinations, remains to be seen.

The Implications for Managerial Strategies

The population changes and their dynamics are so sweeping and so pervasive as to affect all institutions, businesses and public service institutions alike. But because they are so far-ranging in their changes, population dynamics will also affect each institution and even each business differently.

The new segmentation in the consumer market may be of no importance to a machine-tool manufacturer; but production sharing may be crucial to him. To the hospital administrator, production sharing is quite unimportant; the bedpans of a hospital in Detroit or Duesseldorf must be emptied in Detroit or Duesseldorf, which means that the costs for the least-skilled work in hospitals will go up the most in developed countries. The two-income family may however have major impact on the American hospital: it may sharply cut the radius within which the hospital can expect to attract customers. The mother of a hospitalized child wants to be with the child or at least visit it twice a day. If not working or working only part time, she is quite willing to travel ten or fifteen miles from her home to be with her child; if she works full time, the radius shrinks to five miles or so, even if gasoline is plentiful, so that she can easily travel on her way to or from work. The extension of lifespan as well as the drop in birthrates have obviously had a major impact on hospital administrations but the buying patterns of retired people or transnational economic integration are no more than incidental information for them.

The changes thus require that every kind of business

institution examine carefully what opportunities they create; what changes in its own definition of its mission they demand; and what shifts in behavior and practices they indicate. The population dynamics represent a major shift in the environment—in the markets of each institution, in its products or services, in the way it organizes itself for performance, and in the way it brings its products or services to the customer.

Even small and purely local businesses may have to learn to think and to operate transnationally. And businesses already in the world economy will have to learn to think and to behave quite differently. The small business operating within a local or regional market may have to learn to organize its production transnationally and by stages of production rather than in one centralized "manufacturing" process; or it may have to learn to buy parts from all over and to assemble when today it buys finished products for resale.

The company already in the world economy faces even more challenging changes in its attitudes, its behavior, and its practices. It will have to learn to look upon the developing countries as potential sources for labor-intensive stages of production. It will have to learn also that the "foreign subsidiary" of the future is likely to be different from that of the nineteenth-century past, especially in developing countries. Its basis is not the local market but the market in the developing countries. It is not a "business" but a "supplier." The question to be asked in respect to it is not: "How much can it sell in its market?" It is: "What is its capacity to produce parts or components for export to be integrated with the marketing system in the developed world?"

Politically, too, the transnational requires a different attitude, different policies, and a different rhetoric. Multinationals in dealing with developing countries have proceeded on the assumption that it is their capital that makes them attractive. Increasingly, the contribution that matters to developing countries will be jobs and export earnings. Capital investment should be kept to a minimum—and not only because it makes the investor the captive of the host country, vulnerable to political or social turmoil. The desirable position for a transnational in developing countries (considering especially those countries' predictable resistance to economic interdependence) is one in which the developing country benefits from the foreigner's ability to market abroad. In fact, this may be the only tenable position.

It may be most desirable to be in a country that has the potential to develop a genuine national market, which then can itself become integrated into the world economy. The most desirable location for production-sharing manufacturing may thus be an "almost-developed country" (see Part 4 below), which is also where the needed foreign managers, professionals, technicians usually prefer to live. But the rationale of operating transnationally—unlike the rationale of yesterday's multinational—is not the market of the developing, the host, country; it is its labor supply. And for the host country, the attraction of the foreigner is not his capital: it is the jobs he creates in work for export, the export earnings he produces, the markets overseas he creates and develops, and finally the development of local people as managers, marketers, professionals, and as themselves schooled in operating in an integrated world economy.

But for many businesses and most public service institutions population dynamics in the home market and in the home society may demand equally innovative thinking—new concepts, attitudes, policies, and practices.

From "Labor Force" to "Labor Forces"

Governments and government statistics, backed up by economists and managers, still speak of the "labor force." But this term is becoming misleading. More and more there are "labor forces," each with different expectations, different needs, and different characteristics. These forces are affected quite differently by economic and social developments such as a depression. It can only cause trouble to treat them as a homogeneous entity, as most personnel policies and benefit plans do, and as labor unions all insist on doing.

The Misleading Unemployment Figures

Every developed country still adheres to one unemployment figure. Typically, as in the United States, it was designed to measure the number of adult male heads of household out of work. But this group is now a minority of the total labor force everywhere in the West. The figures we use are thus quite misleading and are misinterpreted everywhere. Most Americans reading the monthly "unemployment" figure assume automatically that it reports the number of experienced adult men who have held full-time jobs and are actively looking for a full-time job. Yet most people reported as "unemployed" in the American figures are not adult men, never held a full-time job before, and are not even available for full-time work, let alone looking for it.

Governments cannot reform unemployment figures; they have become the sacred cows of the labor movement. But businessmen can at least learn how to read them. In the American economy there are three sets of employment figures that a businessman needs to look at and from which he needs to take his guidance.

There is first the figure of *labor force participation*, both in numbers and percentage of the labor force. It is no accident that the much-vaunted "recession" of 1973–74 produced no reduction in consumer buying. For during that period, except in two quarters, both the labor force participation and the total number of Americans with jobs were going up and up and up. These figures are the only true and reliable indices of consumer purchasing power.

The second meaningful figure is *the number of male adult heads of household employed and unemployed*. These workers are a minority of the total labor force in members, but they contribute the bulk of the hours worked in the economy. They contribute the overwhelming majority, both of full-time workers and of skilled workers. They are also still everywhere the main providers of "family income," especially in the lower income groups. Their employment or unemployment is thus the most reliable index of labor market and wage pressures.

In the United States, during that "recession" of 1973–74, the number and proportion of fully employed male adult heads of household went down for four months only. For the rest of the period it was steadily rising. Also during that period it stood consistently above the "full employment rate" of 96 percent. In other words, during almost the entire period of supposedly high unemployment, the United States economy actually experienced a substantial labor shortage— as anyone who tried to hire a machinist or a tool setter soon found out.

Finally, there is the official but purely political figure of "*unemployment*," which is meaningless, indeed misleading for business and economic policy, but which determines the intensity of rhetoric and the intensity of political pressures.

Henceforth, executives in all developed countries will have to be able to understand the complexity of employment and unemployment figures. And if they have to choose any one figure to steer by, it should be the employment or unemployment figure for male heads of household, which is closest in meaning to what unemployment figures in the United States, as well as in western Europe, are supposed to measure.

The Need for Different Personnel Policies

Businessmen cannot, I repeat, change the misleading unemployment figures; they can only learn to read them correctly. But they can change personnel policies in their enterprises, which tend to be as much out of date and as misdirecting as the unemployment figures. In most institutions personnel policies are based on the assumption of a homogeneous work force, and primarily, of course, of a work force that consists of adult male heads of household working full time and dependent entirely on their wage or salary from one employer for their livelihood and that of their family. (Exceptions, for example the British provision for employed married women to opt out of parts of National Insurance, are quite rare.)

This group is by now, however, a minority in all developed countries (except maybe Japan). Even the male adult working full time is, in growing numbers and proportions, not the "head of household" but a "partner" in a two-income family. Yet under our present personnel policies, both he and his working spouse are enrolled in a number of benefit plans—on the assumption that both are the "breadwinners" and that therefore the entire family has to be covered by the benefit plans of each. Increasingly, there are working women, both full time and part time, some of whom are "heads of household" and others married to a working husband and considered "dependents." There are people who have "retired" from one job with a pension and then work for another employer, full time or part time. The list could be continued; these are only some of the main groups.

Employers—whether governments, businesses, or nonprofit institutions—are going to have to develop different personnel policies for these different employe groups.

It makes little sense to subject all employes to training programs, to personnel policies, and to supervision designed for one group of employes, and in particular designed, as so many of the policies are, for yesterday's typical entrant into the labor force—the fifteen- or sixteen-year-old without any experience. More and more we will need to have personnel policies that fit the person rather than bureaucratic convenience or tradition.

Industry and government have not yet learned to look upon the labor market as a market to which they have to sell their jobs. And yet jobs are just as much a "product" as toasters or shoes or magazines, and need to be marketed to the potential customer.

The mature woman who applies for a job in the office or the plant after having raised her children has been a "chief executive officer" at home for ten years or more. No one told her whether to dust first or to make the beds first—and both chores got done. Yet when she starts working, she is put under a "supervisor" who treats her as a moron who has never done anything on her own before when what she needs is a teacher and an assistant. Similarly, the older people who have retired from their jobs and now go on to work full time or part time elsewhere know how to work—indeed, they often go to work because that is the only thing they know how to do. But their knowledge, maturity, and experience are not used in existing personnel policies. No one asks: "What can you do?" Instead, they are put into a "training class," together with the sixteen-year-old high school dropout.

The rules of some orders of Catholic nuns are extreme examples of how not to proceed. The orders are dying out because they cannot recruit new members. Most of them experienced, in the sixties and seventies, a sizable increase in the number of applicants, but the dropout rates, which were minimal earlier, increased even faster. To be sure, few young women applied for entry into a religious order—there are too many other choices. But there is a growing number of deeply religious Catholic women, teachers or nurses, who at age fifty are afraid of being alone and lonely and then want to become nuns. The order subjects them to the same training it used to give a fifteen-year-old without schooling or work experience. No wonder these women then protest: "I have been looking after my brother's children for twenty years. I have been running the fourth grade in school or the night shift at the hospital. I know how to sew—I made all the clothes for my brother's children for twenty years. But when I applied for admission to the nuns, they put me into an elementary sewing class and gave me a three-hour lecture on how to boil water."

—And for Benefit Options

As a result of one hundred years of brainwashing by labor leaders, employers have come to believe in uniform benefits. They all complain about their cost. The "fringes" today are almost as wide as the base wage itself. Yet much of the money conveys little benefit to the intended recipient.

The married woman whose husband has a health insurance plan at his place of work receives no benefit from her health insurance. However, one way or another, 8 to 10 percent of her salary is withheld. (For even if the employer pays 100 percent, the money still comes out of the only available pocket, that of the employe.) The same woman pays 6 to 8 percent of her income into a company pension plan from which she is unlikely ever to receive a penny, if only because, as a married woman, she is unlikely to stay around long enough to qualify. Above all, she has to pay full Social Security. Yet under the American system—and other countries are none too different—she will be better off, twenty years hence, to apply for old age benefits as the dependent of her husband, than to apply for benefits on the basis of her own earnings. One way or another, the pension systems of all developed countries share the same bias against the married working woman.

What is urgently needed is a benefits policy that accepts the heterogeneity of the labor force in the period of population changes. "Benefit" to one employe is only cost to another.

The proportion of wage and salary any one employer is willing and able to put aside for employe benefits should be the same for every employe, or for every category of employes. But where the money goes should depend upon the needs, the circumstances, the family situation, the life cycle of the individual employe. The benefits policy should take the form of a set of options, from which the individual employe can choose the total package that gives him or her the most for the money available. The choice as to which benefits are the right ones for this or that individual is then best made by the individual alone.

This idea is anathema to union leaders, who depend on uniformity and who therefore subordinate the majority of members to the largest single minority. It is anathema to government bureaucrats, who always believe they know best what is good for the individual. It will also be resisted by employers, who think that administrative convenience is the ultimate criterion of benefits and of personnel policies all told. But it will be increasingly necessary. Indeed, the employes themselves in the developed countries are going to insist that they be given freedom of choice as to what benefits are optimal for them: freedom of choice on second careers; freedom of choice as to whether to retire at a given age or to stay on working; freedom of choice very largely in their job assignments as well. This is, after all, the essence of being a knowledge worker—and increasingly it will be the knowledge workers who will determine, in the developed countries, the shape of personnel and benefit policies to come.

The End of Mandatory Retirement Age

In all developed countries, it will become a matter of economic survival that retirement age be postponed and that retirement be made flexible and a matter of personal decision. Society and economy simply cannot support the number of people who would otherwise have to be supported. And the older people will increasingly resist being retired and will have the power to enforce their will.

In the United States in 1935, there were eleven people at work for every person over sixty-five; today the ratio is three to one. It will be close to two to one by 1990. Economists will point out that this tremendous increase in the number of "dependent" people of old age is offset to some extent by the sharp drop in the number of children. But this is irrelevant politically, socially, and economically—it is indeed a fallacy. The worker who receives an amount of money in his paycheck and who then has to pay for his children's shoes does not feel that he is paying for an "alien" or even a "dependent." He is paying for his own family. The worker who has the same amount of money withheld from his paycheck to pay for somebody who is now retired feels—with good reason—that this is compulsory taxation and that money he has earned is being forcibly taken away.

The people at work are going to resist paying for others who are not at work although they are physically and mentally capable of being so. Equally, the growing number of older people will become an unbearable burden if they retire; will be resented and resisted.

Unless we extend working-age life one way or another, we will also be building inflationary pressure into the economy of every developed country. Older people tend to consume rather than to save. The money that is being transferred from the paychecks of the younger people at work into retirement pay for older people therefore becomes inflationary purchasing power. The younger people in turn will generate inflationary pressures as they demand that their incomes be raised so as to compensate them for what is being taken away to pay for the older people. In other words, the dependency ratio will become unbearable.

In every developed country, it will have to be a central aim of economic and social policy to keep the ratio between people retired for age and people working at around three to one. This means that in all developed countries the actual retirement age, the age at which people can be expected to stop working, is likely to be closer to seventy-two by the year 1995 than it is to the sixty-five of traditional Western retirement, let alone to the fifty-five of the Japanese tradition. It will make little difference whether the old people work "legally" or in the "gray economy," as long as they work at least part time.

But the major force toward an extension of working life will not be economics. It will be the need of older people who are physically and mentally "young" to keep busy, to have something to do, to get out of the house, and to be productive.

In *The Unseen Revolution: How Pension Fund Socialism Came to America,* I predicted that by the mid-1980s mandatory retirement age in the United States would be raised from sixty-five to seventy. This was considered the height of absurdity by almost every critic. Mandatory retirement in the United States, everyone then said, would be sharply lowered. There was indeed a labor union proposal before Congress to lower compulsory retirement age to sixty or sixty-two; and everyone—government, labor unions, economists, and employers, whether businessmen or university presidents—was bitterly opposed. Yet twelve months after my book appeared, a bill was passed in the California legislature to outlaw mandatory retirement at any age altogether. Shortly thereafter, the Congress of the United States—again against determined and organized opposition by all "respectable" people—eliminated any mandatory retirement age for federal government employes and raised it to seventy for everybody else; and Congress, everybody concedes, will soon eliminate mandatory retirement altogether as California has already done. In part this was the result of pressure from the older people, a pressure that will become more potent. For the older people—and in this context this means everybody over fifty-five who is conscious of the approach of traditional retirement age—are by themselves in developed countries a near-majority of the voting population, if only because their voting participation is so much higher than that of voters under thirty-five. In part, of course, the raising or abolition of mandatory retirement age was simply a response to inexorable economics.

In Europe, the trend still strongly runs in the other direction. In almost every European country, there are proposals to lower compulsory retirement age. Only Japan is willing to accept the logic of population dynamics. There, retirement age is now being pushed up to age sixty, whereas actually the Japanese retirement age should be seventy—if there is to be one at all—to accord with the realities of Japanese life expectancies.

But, whatever legislators and trade unions decide, an increasing number of older people are going to be neither willing nor able to "retire," and they will continue to participate one way or another in the work force. Everywhere—in the United States, in western Europe, in Japan, and in the Soviet bloc—the proportion of older people who are officially retired but who actually work at least part time is steadily growing. One indication is the steady growth of the "black" or "gray labor market," or "moonlighting": people who work full time or part time but do not report their earnings to the tax collector.

The head of Britain's Inland Revenue estimated in the spring of 1979 that 7.5 percent of the country's true national income was never reported to the tax collector and therefore never shown in England's national income statistics. For Sweden I have heard estimates that go up to 20 percent, or one-fifth of the total national income. In the United States, the government's General Accounting Office recently estimated the unreported income from "moonlighting" at 10 percent of personal income.

Resistance to confiscatory taxes surely plays a part in this phenomenon, especially in countries like Sweden with tax rates of more than 100 percent on earnings above a certain fairly low maximum. But people who are officially "retired" also must figure heavily among the "moonlighters" or "black workers." In most countries, people who are officially retired are either not supposed to work at all, as in Great Britain or Sweden, are under labor union pressure not to work, or, as in the United States and the United Kingdom, have their retirement pay taken away altogether or at least severely cut. Consequently, these people report officially that they are indeed "retired," and work as "moonlighters" or "black workers" without telling authority about it.

The resistance to compulsory retirement is going to be greatly accentuated by the educational shift in the work force. Eight out of every ten people who reach the traditional American retirement age of sixty-five these days had only a junior high school education, whereas six out of every ten new entrants into the labor force from now on will have had formal schooling beyond high school. The people who retire have largely worked in manual jobs all their lives; the people who come in are primarily available for skilled work. Manual workers, by and large, are content to retire at age fifty-five or sixty, after thirty-five years in the steel mill. To be sure, a large minority, perhaps a majority, then start working again—in part because it is boring to spend all the time fishing or sitting on the front porch of a mobile home chatting with the neighbors; in part because they need to earn extra money, although they feel no psychological urge to report these extra earnings to a tax collector.

For knowledge workers, however, the need to keep on doing something productive is overwhelming.

The Need for a Second Career

This need on the part of the knowledge worker not to "retire" at any given age will lead to seeking a second career in his or her forties or fifties. It is not easy to find a new job at sixty-five if one has never before changed careers. But any type of knowledge work palls if done too long. Our institutions are full of people in their forties who are bored, having done the same work for too long.

The worst offenders are perhaps the university faculties, for the simple reason that they are our most restrictive employers. The young scholar who starts teaching the French Revolution loves his subject; fifteen years later, though still only in his early forties, he is bored with it. The one book he had in him has long ago been written; now he agonizes over two book reviews a year. His lectures are repetitious; even his jokes are stale, though the kids still dutifully laugh. But the rules of academia make it all but impossible for him to teach other periods in history, let alone to move out of the History Department altogether.

The hospital is equally restrictive, with no transfer available for an X-ray technician into physical therapy or medical technology. Even business, while by far the most flexible environment and the one with the most mobility, still tends to keep a manager or professional in one area of work and in one surrounding until he is bored. He is not "burnt out," but he does need to be put into a different environment to meet different challenges, to be "re-potted." He needs a second career. He needs a new environment, with new associates and new challenges.

As a result of the growing pressure for second careers, the continuing education of already highly educated adults will expand in the years ahead. Equally important will be the systematic placement of accomplished middle-aged executives—especially middle-level executives—in new jobs with new tasks and new challenges.

The Japanese, despite their emphasis on "lifetime employment" and on "loyalty" to one company (or perhaps because of it), actually do a better job at providing second careers for executives than either Europe or the United States. The Japanese company moves managerial people from one functional job to another without much regard for a man's previous experience or formal training. It does not hesitate to put a sales manager into accounting or an engineering manager into personnel. In this way the senior people in a large Japanese company usually have been exposed to more stimuli and to greater variety than the typical American or European executive, who tends to stay all his working life in one area.

To sum up, the employer of tomorrow will have to learn to use full-time people and part-time people, men and women, people past retirement age and people who are interested only in working in one functional or technical skill (such as today's computer specialists) and who move on to a different employer once they have finished a particular assignment. Whether university, hospital, or business, the employer will have to move from managing personnel to managing people.

The "Double-Headed Monster"

An old saying goes, "One cannot run a hospital with doctors, and one cannot run one without them." Similarly, every university administrator has said, if only to himself, "One cannot run a university with the faculty but one cannot, alas, run one without it either." This applies to all modern organizations, including the business enterprise. All enterprises are becoming "double-headed monsters," which depend for their performance on professionals who are dedicated to their discipline rather than to the institution, who are the more productive the more dedicated they are, and who, at the same time, have to work toward the accomplishment of the goals of the whole. The emergence of the "double-headed monster" is also the result of population dynamics. It is yet another example of turbulent times that managers have to learn to manage.

Professionals have always resisted attempts to hold them accountable. It is the essence of being a professional—so the doctor, lawyer, engineer, or priest has always argued—that one is not accountable to laymen and that qualification rather than performance is the ground of acceptance. This was so, but today it is no longer tenable. It worked as long as the professionals were a small fringe without whom society could get along perfectly well. In modern society, however, the "professionals"—or people who see themselves as possessors of a distinct organized knowledge and primarily accountable to it—are the very center of society and of its performance capacity. They are no longer an ornament, a luxury. And their claim that they justify themselves by their diploma, the traditional claim of the professional, is no longer valid. Society must demand that these people think through what they should be held accountable for and that they take responsibility for their contribution.

The standard response is that the contribution of the professional is not "measurable." But the output of the manual worker was not "measurable" either 150 years ago, before Frederick W. Taylor started his task study, which made manual work capable of measurement. It is reasonable to assume that professional work can at least be made capable of being judged. In measurement, the result one person obtains should be obtainable by anybody else who uses the same measuring stick. In judgment, the result an informed and qualified person obtains is supposedly going to be reached by any other qualified and informed person. Judgment presupposes information and some expertise, but is otherwise as "objective" as is measurement. We should be able to judge the performance of professionals and are, in fact, perfectly capable of doing so.

In the American hospital, the medical profession is now being asked to examine the standards of good medical care for a given group of diseases or complaints and then to police within its own medical community the observance by the practitioners of these standards. This, it is hoped, will actually be done within the profession, so that the physician who chooses a different mode of practice must explain his actions to a fellow physician who heads a certain service. But if the professionals are unwilling or unable to impose this discipline upon themselves, American society will surely impose it upon them—with laymen, such as hospital administrators, then actually becoming the "bosses" of the profession. The legal profession is moving in the same direction. And the demand that teachers think through and spell out what society, taxpayers, and parents should expect from their performance in the classroom, and then hold themselves accountable for reaching these goals, is rapidly gaining ground as well.

It is no longer a question whether professionals should be held accountable. The question is only whether they will develop their own standards or have standards imposed upon them.

This transformation of institutions into "double-headed monsters" in which there is both a business management and professional groups (whether accountants, market researchers, salesmen, engineers, or quality control people) will force us into new, and fairly radical, organizational concepts. Business organization as we know it has developed fundamentally in the shape of a pyramid, with a "command" function, mitigated by the emergence of "staffs" who were "advisory" rather than "command." Increasingly, the hospital or the university will be a better model than the traditional military, perhaps even for the military itself. Increasingly, we will see organizations as concentric, overlapping, coordinated rings, rather than as pyramids. There is need for "top management" and there is need for an ultimate "command"—just as there is need for a skeleton in the animal body. There is need for a clear locus of decisions, for a clear voice and for unity of command in the event of common danger and emergencies. But there is also need for accepting that within given fields the professionals should set the standards and determine what their contribution should be.

Top management can, in effect, cut out the training program. But it cannot tell the trainer how to train. All it can do is get another trainer if it feels that the present one does not know his job. The university president may decide to increase the budget for foreign languages or reduce it. But he cannot tell the language faculty how to teach foreign languages, and perhaps not even which ones to teach. The hospital administrator, whether he has a medical degree or not, may decide to add fifteen beds in clinical neurology. But what then constitutes good clinical neurology is not within the administrator's purview. He can only demand that the neurologists think through what their objectives are, what their standards are, and how they propose to make effective their individual and collective accountability for the practice of clinical neurology within his hospital.

But it is the administrator who has to make sure that the professional people do indeed take accountability, develop standards, set goals, and rigorously judge their performance against these standards and goals.

This means that organizational structures are going to look different in the future. A well-known university president once said: "There is no top management in this university. Every professor, certainly every senior professor, is at least as much 'top management' as I am—and not one of us can make decisions." This is one way to describe the modern institution. But another is the way a major book publisher talked of his company: "There is only top management in this firm, except for the messenger boys." This too is an apt description; it is in fact how a book publishing house has to work if authors are to be willing to entrust their works to it. Both definitions are clearly right. In other words, the organization in its internal environment is going to be as pluralist as the external environment in which it lives. And the transition from the traditional pyramid to the "double-headed monster" is another shift to be managed as population structure and population dynamics change.

Job Needs in the Developing Countries

Population dynamics are changing the priorities of and restraints on social policy—in developing countries as much as in developed ones. They will force managers to take the lead in changing widely held beliefs, in changing priorities, and in formulating new policies of job and income security, different alike from both the Western approaches of unemployment compensation and punitive restrictions on laying off people and the Japanese "lifetime employment."

In the developing world, the first priority will be to create jobs for the large masses of young people. This will have to take precedence over nationalist pride and traditional beliefs, slogans, sentiments, and resentments. It is a matter of survival—and survival has priority.

The businessman from the developed world had better stay away from a developing country that does not accept this priority. It will be too dangerous, for the country will almost certainly neither achieve, perform, nor develop. International institutions such as the World Bank, the Inter-American Development Bank, and the International Monetary Fund will have to learn to demand of their clients in the developing world that they put job creation—and especially job creation in manufacturing processes focused on export to the developed world—at the top of their political and social priorities.

It has been the great strength of those pragmatists the non-Communist Chinese that they saw this earlier than anybody else. The fact that their countries—Hong Kong, Taiwan, Singapore, and culturally-Chinese South Korea—are now "almost developed countries" (see Part 4 below), and that South Korea is expected by many observers to be the next fully developed economic "great power," is the direct result of giving first priority to the creation of jobs in manufacturing for exports, and of subordinating to this goal every other consideration. The extreme example is the free-market and pro-multinational policy of the avowedly "Socialist" government of Singapore.

The economic success of Brazil in the last fifteen years also squarely rests on giving priority to the importance of creating jobs. The Brazilian example shows, however, that there are serious risks. Priority on job creation creates social tension. It entails social inequality. The managerial groups under such a policy must be encouraged to enjoy a standard of income and a way of life similar to the standard of living and way of life of their counterparts in the developed world. Maybe they even need to live somewhat better, if only to attract and hold highly educated people who could do very well for themselves working in the developed world, whether as businessmen, scientists, physicians, or engineers. At the same time, the country has to be competitive in its labor costs and productivity, which means that the "trade-off" for rapid expansion of the number of jobs in manufacturing is keeping wages lagging behind increases in productivity. This causes a high and socially dangerous inequality between still small upper and middle groups and rapidly growing working masses.

The opposite policy, which India has been following—the policy of disregarding job creation as a priority, or at most, of paying lip service to it while slighting it in practice—has proved even more dangerous.

The Indian government faces a real dilemma. It is trying to keep a ceiling on the incomes of educated people. Physicians, engineers, executives, and university professors are not supposed to have a larger yearly after-tax income than $6,000 or $7,000 including benefits and "perks." This is still fifty to one hundred times more than a peasant family in the village is likely to make in a year, and represents an extreme of social inequality in a country where eight out of ten families live in the villages. But the permitted maximum income is a fraction of what a trained or educated Indian can earn outside of India. It is also well below what he needs to live on at a minimum urban middle-class standard, let alone "Western" standards, in a country where modern amenities—housing, a car, schooling, a newspaper, or a book—cost a good deal more than they do in the West. So there is a steady exodus of trained, skilled, educated Indians at every level. And among those who stay, the official policy creates large-scale corruption and pervasive cynicism.

Job creation poses an additional problem. It is not just the number of jobs that matters; it is the number of *productive* jobs. Unproductive or less than fully productive jobs actually inhibit and impede productive employment. In fact, they can destroy jobs.

Again, the non-Communist Chinese societies and South Korea saw this earlier and more clearly than anybody else.

Hong Kong in particular has done an outstanding job. Until the Vietnamese refugees began to inundate the city in 1979, every Chinese immigrant was found a productive job within a few months by the Chinese community itself, with the British colonial government keeping its hands off by and large. The Chinese community, in the Chinese tradition, controls wages closely, although unofficially and through social pressure rather than rules and regulations. Gross exploitation is frowned upon; but so is upward wage pressure that would make Hong Kong less competitive. "Our one yardstick is productivity," a powerful Hong Kong community leader explained. "Workers are entitled to maximum benefit from productivity gains; and employers are obliged to put in the capital equipment and the work methods that enable employes to work 'smarter' and to be more productive. But just as low wages in the presence of productivity harm economy and community, so do high wages without productivity." No doubt this is idealized but it is the right principle. At the same time, Hong Kong has kept very low the "social overhead," that is especially government jobs, as being basically unproductive.

In India over the last few years, there has been a sharp reaction to the uncritical admiration of anything very big, whether nuclear reactor or steel mill, that characterized the earlier years under Nehru. But the opposite emphasis of today's official Indian rhetoric is just as superstitious and deleterious. The Indian government in the last few years has, for instance, tried to ban the mechanical spindle; even the spinning wheel equipped with a set of bicycle pedals which an ingenious Indian invented and which triples the yarn production of the operative is officially forbidden. The only result has been a brisk black market in mechanical spindles bought by small entrepreneurs with the right government connections, and an equally brisk semilegal trade in bicycle pedals bought officially for "replacement." Still the official attitude persists. It was summed up for me by one of the government's most influential economists: "The big mistake Gandhi made was to advocate the spinning wheel. It's much too productive. We need to go back to the distaff; it creates more jobs."

But poor countries cannot afford to support huge masses who do not produce even while twirling a distaff. Only very rich countries can support a welfare population. What

India—and all developing countries—needs are jobs in which the country's own resources are most productively employed. For she needs to be able to compete in a world economy for access to the markets of the developed world.

The "appropriate" technology for any country, whether developed or developing, is not what is biggest or smallest. It is not, as was believed in the 1950s, what absorbs the most capital; that is waste. Nor is it what absorbs the most labor, for this also is waste. What is "appropriate" is what makes available resources most productive—and then also creates the most jobs.

For the next twenty years or so, the investment with the highest "multiplier" effect in developing countries, and the greatest capacity to create productive jobs, will be investment in production sharing, investment in jobs in the labor-intensive stages of manufacturing production, the output of which is being marketed through transnational confederations in the developed world.

Job Needs in the Developed World

The massive reality for the developed countries will be one of labor scarcity rather than labor surplus in the traditional employments, both in manufacturing and in the services. And yet managers in these countries will have to work on creating jobs, and on making existing jobs more meaningful, challenging, and responsible.

For developed countries will not suffer a shortage of educated people, not even of *young* educated people. Instead they will have a surplus during the next ten years, when the last cohorts of the baby-boom birth years come on the labor market and start their careers with high expectations quite at variance with what may be offered to them.

When the baby boom began, and for twenty years thereafter, there was a vacuum in managerial and professional

ranks in the developed countries. Birthrates had been low
from the twenties through the forties, so that the managerial,
professional, and technical population of the early fifties was
thin. It remained so through the sixties and early seventies.

The last period in which American schools, including the
universities, heavily hired young people was the twenties,
when the high schools exploded—only to be hit shortly
thereafter by the combined effects of the Great Depression
and a steady decline in the birthrate. By the mid-1950s the
teaching population in American education was uniformly old.
When the babies of the baby boom began to come in, the
schools, to keep up with the tide, had to hire three people for
every one of the teachers who were retiring. The situation in
American banks was similar; there too, the last period of
substantial hiring had been before 1929.

In German industry, the last period in which large numbers
of people were hired had been around 1925–26. World War II
took a very heavy toll of men in their twenties and thirties; as
a result, there was a vacuum in the 1950s and 1960s. In Japan,
young people went into the armed services rather than into
business and industry from 1934 on; after the war a whole
generation of older people was purged at the top, creating a
vacuum of young educated people in the middle that per-
sisted until the mid-seventies.

Employers in the developed countries had to compete for
whatever young people came out of the schools, and especially out of higher education. The people who graduated
from the university in the sixties and seventies, particularly
the ones who graduated with advanced degrees, made excep-
tionally fast careers.

"I do not know how to allocate the percentages," the
personnel manager of one of New York's major banks comments, "but I think it a fair guess to attribute 50 percent of the
careers of our young upper-level executives to their abilities
and hard work and 50 percent to demographics."

The result is that today we have structures of senior business executives, senior university teachers, senior hospital administrators, and so on, that are heavily biased on the side of youth.

Typically in the large American bank, but also in a good many of the large European banks, an assistant vice president today is twenty-eight or so. He or she has about as many years of life as one traditionally needed to have years of service to attain such rank and title. This assistant vice president then reports to a vice president who is thirty-one, who in turn reports to a senior vice president who is thirty-four, who reports to an executive vice president who is thirty-eight. Similar age structures prevail in academia, in the hospitals, in governmental agencies, and in marketing organizations. In other words, the pipelines are full. Yet the large numbers of young people who will complete advanced and professional training, and graduate with advanced degrees these next years are the younger brothers or sisters of that young assistant vice president at Citibank—or at Deutsche Bank or Banque Nationale de Paris. They will expect, quite reasonably, to make a similar career. But where the older brother or sister a few years ago graduated into a vacuum, the younger educated people reach a market that is well supplied and, in many areas, saturated—as the markets for young lawyers or young surgeons already are in the United States.

For the next five or ten years, employers in all institutions in the developed countries will face frustration among their brightest, most ambitious, most achieving young people. These people will not be able to count, as their immediate predecessors did, on rapid promotion for their satisfaction, reward, and sense of accomplishment. They will need bigger, more challenging tasks.

What kind of tasks will these have to be? What challenges can be built into the new jobs? What do the achievements and satisfactions need to be, to hold and develop a young, able, hardworking, and ambitious person? This will be one of the major management concerns of the next ten years.

Managers and policymakers alike in the developed countries will have to learn that satisfying "job needs" increasingly means creating productive jobs for the knowledge worker, the educated person. This will be true in terms of numbers. For while people willing to work in traditional jobs will increasingly be in short supply (especially people for traditional, skilled and unskilled manual work); people qualified for knowledge work and expecting knowledge jobs will be available and plentiful. The focus on the creation of such jobs and on performance in them will become increasingly important to the developed countries. They cannot possibly hope to compete in terms of traditional labor. Costs are much too high, and such advantages as exist—for example, in Japan in some employments with high automation—are transitory and will be offset by increased productivities in developing countries, with their huge reservoirs of trainable young people eager to acquire traditional competence and traditional skills. The developed countries can only hope to maintain their standard of living, their standard of education, their leadership position, if they put to work productively the only resource in which they have a distinct advantage: their ability to keep young people in school for long years and to qualify them for knowledge work.

This implies that in all developed countries scholastic standards and demands are likely to go up in the next decades. The implication is outside the scope of this book, but should be mentioned in passing if only because the young, perhaps sensing it, are already pushing in this direction. Demographics will also put even greater force behind the shift of the young from such "general" subjects as the social sciences toward "practical knowledge" such as engineering, accounting, or health-care technologies. We can expect even greater impetus to be given to the continuing or postgraduate professional and technical education of these workers in mid-career.

The knowledge jobs in the developed countries will increasingly have to be jobs producing economic value. The developed countries with their high social overhead and high capital costs will have to be able to produce high economic value to maintain their accustomed standards of consumption, of education, and of health care, let alone to increase them. This means, first, that the job growth will again have to be primarily in the economic sector, whether that sector is "free-enterprise," "nationalized," or "mixed." It means, secondly, that demographics alone will demand that the developed countries swing back from macroeconomics, which focuses on demand, to microeconomics, focusing on productivity and supply (see Parts 1 and 2).

Above all, it means that developed countries will have to learn to give priority to production sharing. Only careful planning, organization, integration, and management of production sharing will succeed in producing well-paid, challenging, and achieving jobs for the large numbers of knowledge workers in the developed countries.

Of all the developed countries, Japan alone so far seems to understand this. Japanese economic and social policy, despite all the concern over unemployment of traditional manual workers, is increasingly based on the willingness to "trade off" manual jobs against knowledge jobs, which in the state of Japanese demographics is the right trade-off no matter how unpopular politically. The opposite, and I fear the most damaging, approach seems to be the British one, where first priority is still given to manual jobs in old and decaying industries.

The Need for Redundancy Planning

The new priorities of social policy require something fundamentally new in respect to yesterday's employe, the manual worker: organized anticipation, organized acceleration, and organized planning for redundancy.

In every developed country we need to go beyond both unemployment insurance and lifetime employment. Both are inadequate and increasingly unable to achieve what they were designed to achieve. What is needed is a commitment on the part of management to lifetime jobs in the economy, a commitment which ensures the employe against redundancy caused by structural change, whether economic or technological, but which at the same time maintains (indeed improves) the ability of the economy to change structurally, to adapt, and to innovate.

Developed countries will have to be able to innovate fast. They will have to be able to automate such industrial processes as can be automated or they will simply not be able to maintain their industry. They will have to be able to slough off labor-intensive stages of production and labor-intensive industries. They will have to develop rapidly the new knowledge-intensive stages of production and the knowledge-intensive industries. And they will have to shift fairly rapidly to new sources of energy. In short (as we saw in Part 2), they will have to be able to initiate structural changes. Adaptation alone will not be enough to ensure their prosperity and social cohesion.

The attempt to escape these pressures by traditional means, and especially by traditional protectionism, cannot work. Protectionism transfers purchasing power from consumers to producers; but with the new demographics of the developed countries, this is futile. Traditional protectionism rests on the availability of traditional, i.e., manual, workers.

The problem of the developed countries will not be that their workers cost more and produce less—the condition protectionism subsidizes—but that there will be none to do the work, or certainly not enough of them to do it all.

The American tanning industry, as already mentioned, has lately called for restrictions on the export of American hides to be tanned abroad. But at the same time leaders of the industry identify "the absence of Americans available for work in the tanning industry and willing to do the dirty work involved" as a major obstacle to the survival of the industry in the United States. To be sure, a little more tanning could probably be done in the United States today, though only at much higher cost. But to do enough tanning to produce all or even most of the leather needed for the shoes Americans buy is out of the question. The labor is not available, no matter how protected the tanning industry might be. The same has long been true for merchant ships of traditional pre-automated design, or for clothing manufacture.

And if the labor is not available, protectionism does not just transfer purchasing power. It does not just lower the total standard of living; it does not just "sub-optimize." It impoverishes both producer and consumer and the entire society. It becomes self-defeating.

Yet the need for social continuity persists, especially in a time of rapid change. The developed countries will not be able to adapt fast, let alone to lead, unless they can anticipate and resolve the social problems that the rapid change from a manual-labor force to a knowledge-labor force is creating.

The developed countries cannot afford to do what Great Britain has attempted to do so unsuccessfully and with such disastrous results these last thirty years: try to keep alive yesterday and thereby miss tomorrow (with the Conservatives, by the way, just as guilty as Labour and just as deluded). But they can also not pretend that there is no problem. The problem is a fairly small one, but it is real. And it has to be dealt with.

The population dynamics of the developed countries pose the central problem of our turbulent times. They are, in Shakespeare's term, the "sea-change." They will have to be managed, and managed by managers in institutions rather than left to governments or politicians. As a "social problem" encompassing the entire economy, the change may seem unmanageable; but on the local level, the level of the individual company, the individual university, the individual industry, the individual city or region, the problem is comparatively small, relatively easily managed, and reasonably inexpensive to solve.

The workers in the American shoe industry whose jobs are being threatened by production sharing constitute perhaps 60,000 people—or about one-half of one tenth of 1 percent of an employed labor force of 100 millions. Of these 60,000 people, a substantial number are no problem. There are, to start with, quite a few in that group who are ready for early retirement; and every employe over fifty-five in American manufacturing industry has, in his Social Security alone, an early retirement plan that is at least a foundation for economic survival. A second fairly large group are younger workers with less than ten years seniority in the industry. They are, as a rule, perfectly able to find another job, though they may need placement help, counselling, advice, and perhaps a small resettlement loan. So the hard-core "problem" are those workers—probably around half of the total—who are between thirty and fifty-five, with families, with homes, and no experience, as a rule, except in the shoe industry. They are unlikely to be the most accomplished, most mobile, venturesome people; such are rarely attracted to decaying industries, nor do they stay in them. They are concentrated in a few places—people in decaying industries or obsolescent occupations almost always are. And so, though their numbers are small, they are highly visible, have strong political impact (after all, every congressional or parliamentary district is always a "swing" district in which a very small majority of the voters can change the outcome of an election) and can block and veto. And individually they matter.

If one goes by statistics alone, there appears to be no need to be concerned. Statistically, the overwhelming majority of people (even those over fifty-five) find work within a year or two, that is, during the period over which unemployment insurance carries them.

The most recent example is that of Youngstown, Ohio, a steel town that lost its one large employer when the steel mill was shut down. Youngstown was the supreme example of a one-industry town with a helpless, immobile, uninformed population; almost none of the laid-off workers had ever worked for anyone else before. No other major employer has come to town. Yet thirty-six months after the big mill closed, four out of every five of its workers had found other employment; not admittedly all as well paid as the job at the steel mill had been, and a good many on part-time work, but still with jobs to support themselves and their families.

The main point, surely, is that the problem is not so much economic as psychological. What creates resistance to technological or structural change is fear: fear of the unknown, fear of being lost, of being alone, of being an outcast. It is precisely because the problem is not economically unsurmountable—unless a whole region goes down the drain, as did the Welsh collieries in the 1920s, when the coal gave out, or the anthracite mines in Pennsylvania a few years later—that organized planning for redundancy makes so much sense. And it is precisely because the real problem is fear of the unknown, fear of being abandoned in a world the worker does not know or understand, that such organized planning is so badly needed.

To take the American shoe industry again, the beneficiaries of production sharing in the industry outnumber the workers threatened by it at least ten to one. There are more than 500,000 livestock growers and their families in the country whose profit is the hides and who depend on their being tanned and converted into leather at a price at which they can compete in the world market. There are at least another 500,000 employes of shoe wholesalers and shoe retailers who are dependent on shoe sales. But they are spread over the country rather than concentrated; and the benefit of production sharing is indirect and largely hidden from them. Unless the small number of shoe workers in North Carolina can be freed of their fear of structural redundancy, they will veto and block any change.

The traditional approaches do not solve the problem. Both the Western approach of unemployment insurance and the Japanese approach of "lifetime employment" are inadequate; and the more recent one, punitive restrictions on redundancy, does positive harm and aggravates the problem.

Unemployment insurance does give high economic protection. But it has failed to produce what its original inventors, the British, fifty years ago were rightly most concerned with: psychological security. Lifetime employment in Japan has created that security—even though no more than a minority of Japanese employes ever enjoyed it because women, by definition, are not considered "permanent employes" and are thus excluded, and only employes of governments and large businesses (and then only those under fifty-five) are entitled to it among the male workers. But while lifetime employment has given high psychological security, it has also introduced great structural rigidity that is accentuated by the traditional Japanese "seniority wage" structure, which, in effect, makes a worker virtually unemployable if he loses his job once he is more than five or seven years older than the "entrance age" of sixteen for manual workers, nineteen for clerical workers, and twenty-two for managerial and professional workers.

A third approach is becoming more popular in western Europe and is currently being promoted in the United States: to make redundancies so expensive that they will be slowed down or stopped altogether.

Belgium may have gone furthest in this direction. To lay off an employe in Belgium requires "separation pay," which in effect means paying an employe the full salary for the rest of his or her life after ten years of employment. This does indeed prevent people being laid off. But for every person whose job is thus saved, two or three are not being hired. No one in Belgium starts a new business. Some businesses I know need up to 20 percent more employes but hire no one at all. And some Belgian economists—themselves Socialists, close to the Belgian labor unions—estimate that all of Belgian unemployment, which is the highest in western Europe, is caused by the fear of redundancy liability.

In South America, where redundancy payments of this kind originated, either they are evaded by firing the employe two days before he has been on the payroll long enough to qualify, and then rehiring him two weeks later (substituting in effect an unpaid two-weeks layoff for redundancy payments), or, as in Argentina, businesses simply do not hire. In this case, the redundancy payments, as in Belgium, create the very disease they were designed to alleviate or to prevent.

What is wrong with the Belgian system is not the concept but the execution. We do need to provide the employe—and especially the middle-aged manual worker with limited mobility, limited knowledge of the world, and limited horizons—

with the assurance of permanent employment. But we need to do it in such a way as to encourage structural change rather than to penalize it, and so as to create mobility rather than to inhibit it.

The problem has actually been solved twice in simple and effective ways. After the Russo-Japanese War of 1904–5, when the fledgling Japanese manufacturing industry found itself in its first depression, the chief executive of the Mitsui Group required of all Mitsui Group companies that they inform the head office as early as possible of impending layoffs, but also of any need for additional personnel. The Group's head office would then place the redundant employes of one company in the vacancies at another company. The new employer would pay the wage befitting the new employe's seniority in his new job, the entrance wage. The old employer would make up the difference between the entrance wage and the wage befitting the employe's age and length of service with the Mitsui Group. And both the old and the new employer would share the costs of retraining and relocating the employe and his family.

Another far more ambitious and even more successful policy to anticipate redundancies, speed them up, and make them into an actual benefit and opportunity for the employe was fashioned in Sweden thirty years ago. The labor leader Gösta Rehn realized the urgent need for Sweden to change from a pre-industrial, raw-material-producing economy into a modern high-technology one. A very large number of Swedish employes were thus going to be structurally redundant, and had to be prepared for new and very different jobs. Rehn organized around 1950 in each Swedish region a tripartite group, composed of representatives of the employers, the labor unions, and the government, whose task it was to anticipate redundancies at least two years ahead and then to retrain the employes for new jobs. If need be, this group even refinanced the relocation of employes and moved them and their families to the new job. The policy succeeded admirably—unemployment in Sweden was nonexistent as long as the Rehn Plan operated, until 1970 or so. Yet almost half the Swedish labor force became redundant and was placed in new and different jobs. The costs of the Rehn Plan were minimal, well below what unemployment compensation costs in the Western countries that rely on it.

What is needed is a clear, open, and firm commitment to the livelihood, productive employment, and placement of people. This should not be an unlimited commitment. Employes with less than ten years of employment in an industry do not need it; they are young enough to place themselves. Nor do people who are old enough for early retirement need it; they have the financial foundation for economic security. But for manual and clerical workers aged thirty to fifty-five or sixty we need a commitment to job security which, at the same time, is a commitment to anticipating redundancies, to retraining people, and to placing them. It is not a matter of money, as the Swedish example shows. It is primarily a matter of vision and of leadership. But without it, the economies of the developed countries— whether free-market or Communist—will not be able to adapt to the changes of tomorrow. The economic opportunities will instead become monstrous threats to them.

Redundancy planning must be a cooperative venture. The employes must take part in it—and where there is a union, it will surely insist on being a participant too. But the initiative has to be taken by management, for only the management of a particular company, a particular university, a particular hospital can anticipate redundancies ahead, a few years out. Redundancy planning is a major responsibility of management, a major task in managing turbulence. Redundancy planning also should be embraced as a major opportunity for effective leadership in enterprise, community, and society.

4

Managing in Turbulent Environments

Managing in Turbulent Environments

In three related facets of its environment—the economic, the social, and the political—management faces new realities, new challenges, and new uncertainties. Economically, the world has become integrated and interdependent as never before. There is now a true world economy, which is moving toward a transnational money that is increasingly independent of—or at least "uncoupled" from—any national currency. There is no more "key currency." The traditional concept of economic sovereignty, which so very recently seemed to have achieved its ultimate triumph in Keynesian economics, is fast becoming a mockery. While the world economy is increasingly integrated, the world polity is, however, increasingly fragmented; and the process of political disintegration has clearly not run its course. Yet the less effective power governments have, the more do they assert their control.

Socially, one of the true innovations of this century is the employe society. In every developed country, business, especially large business, is being run for the benefit of the wage and salary earners, the employes. Practically the entire national product is paid out to them as wages and salaries. In the world's leading "capitalist" country, the United States, the employes through their pension funds have become the only "capitalists" and the dominant owners of the country's large businesses. The United States has socialized big business without nationalizing it. Yet so far there is no employe responsibility commensurate to employe power, and no social institutions expressing the reality of employe ownership. At the same time, where "employes" yesterday meant "proletarians," today it increasingly means a highly educated professional middle class. It means knowledge workers rather than manual workers. But so far there has been no move to making the employe responsible in line with both his ownership and his status. The legitimacy of management, and of labor union as well, is thus being challenged; it is in transition and seriously in jeopardy.

Finally, the political system in every developed country has become pluralist. Society in all developed countries has become a society of institutions. The political process in every developed country—probably even in totalitarian ones—is moving from integration to confrontation. This makes every institution, including business enterprise, into a political institution that has to attract and to satisfy a number of "constituencies" (i.e., groups accepted as entitled to a say, or at least a veto, even though they may have little or no stake in the institution's primary mission and purpose). Managers therefore have to add a political dimension to their task. They must become activists in politics, who take the initiative, set goals, and create vision rather than being content to cooperate, respond, and react.

These environmental challenges demand new policies, many of them quite radical ones; they create new top management responsibilities, in small and medium-sized as well as large enterprises.

The Integrated World Economy

In the early 1970s, the United States under President Nixon abandoned the dollar as a "key currency." It opted for floating exchange rates for the dollar, and this meant floating exchange rates for all other currencies as well. Since then, the foreign exchange rates of domestic currencies have been openly and brazenly used almost everywhere as tools of domestic politics and are being manipulated to attain short-term economic or even shorter-term political advantages at home. Money, instead of being the standard of value, has become in almost every developed country a "wild card" in political, social, and economic games.

Since the early seventies, when floating exchange rates became the new orthodoxy, there have been two schools of economic thought. The majority of economists, at least in the English-speaking countries, believe that floating exchange rates are here to stay, are desirable and indeed necessary, and that any attempt to return to fixed exchange rates would bring immediate catastrophe.

The minority—a respectably large one—asserts the opposite. Floating exchange rates, the minority maintains, only encourage governments to be profligate. They only create and export inflation. They only lure governments into economic policies that are deleterious even in the short run, let alone the long one. Above all, they withdraw the last remaining economic discipline on government and thus encourage government to become demagogic, irresponsible, inflationary. The world has to return to fixed exchange rates, the minority argues, and to do so soon.

Transnational World Money

The two views seem to be incompatible. And yet the world economy is halfway toward institutionalizing both. The Communist countries, with their monopoly of foreign trade and foreign exchange, have long had a two-tier currency system: a domestic currency, which is completely manipulated within; and a foreign currency, which is completely insulated from the domestic economy. Now the non-Communist developed world is in the process of establishing a two-tier currency system as well. The system increasingly consists of domestic currencies, which are manipulated by government for short-term political ends at home; and of a world currency of account, which is no longer denominated in any one national currency. World economy and world trade are increasingly financed by money that is grounded in purchasing power rather than in any one national currency. But the domestic economy of each country and its trade are conducted in money that is progressively subordinated to the domestic policy, if not to the superstitions, of the moment. Both the floating-rate currency advocated by the majority and the fixed-rate currency advocated by the minority are becoming actual reality. What is being given up is the universally held axiom of the last three hundred years: that there is but one money in any country, and that money, of necessity, has to be based on a national currency with the legal backing of the sovereign behind it.

World trade has been primarily financed by non-governmental bank money for at least a decade now. In the 1950s, the Soviet State Bank invented the "Eurodollar." Afraid of having its American dollar deposits frozen in the event of a confrontation between the Soviet Union and the United States, it withdrew its dollar balances from New York and deposited them with London banks instead. Ten years later, when President Johnson ordered American businesses to stop investing dollars abroad—in a futile bid to appease General de Gaulle, with his obsessive fear of the takeover of Europe by American multinationals—the world economic community adopted this "Eurodollar" as its money of account. To Eurodollars have since been added Euromarks, Euroyen, Euro-Swissfrancs, and so on. The textbooks still define a "Eurodollar" as an American dollar owned by a non-American and on deposit outside the United States. But this became fiction long ago. Eurodollar, Euroyen, Euromark, or Euro-Swissfranc are owned by anybody and deposited anywhere.

They are purely money of account, purely bank money. Yet they have increasingly become the real money of the world economy, receiving their greatest boost from the OPEC cartel with its tremendous liquid funds, which have been fueling the world banking system since 1973.

By now, the Eurocurrencies amount to around $1,000 billion. If loans between banks are excluded, they still come to some $600 or $700 billion, which is more than the total liquid resources in all the currencies of the developed countries. In other words, Eurocurrencies, those completely metaphysical entities, are the true circulatory medium of the world economy.

Back in 1965, when the Eurodollar first emerged as the world's trading money, it could be held that the dollar would remain stable and that the American government could be trusted to follow a responsible monetary policy. That was the reason, of course, why the Eurocurrency was linked to the American dollar. Both assumptions, however axiomatic they may have sounded in 1965, are hardly rational in 1980. And thus the main holders of Eurocurrencies, the main suppliers of liquid funds to the world's credit markets, increasingly demand that their deposits be made independent of the vagaries of American domestic policy and of American currency manipulation. They must demand that their deposits be linked to units of purchasing power rather than dollars, in order to become insulated against depreciation and inflation.

The bulk of the liquid reserves in the world economy is held by exporting manufacturers, especially those based on countries with large trade surpluses such as Japan and Germany, and by the countries of the OPEC petroleum cartel. The positions and problems of the two groups are completely different. But both must try to hold their liquid funds in transnational money, which is not tied to any one currency.

Exporters from countries with large export surpluses are endangered in their existence—or at least in their solvency—by the instability of national currencies, and especially by the instability of the dollar. Their obligations are, of necessity, largely in the countries from which they export, countries with payments surpluses and thus relatively strong currencies. Their income is largely in currencies that are either inherently weak or deliberately manipulated to be weak for domestic political reasons, as the American dollar was in the first years of the Carter administration. They can hedge to some extent against their currency exposure, but there are fairly narrow limits to the amount of hedging the foreign exchange markets can handle. Also hedging is considered "speculation." It is not so, of course; indeed, not to hedge in a period of currency instability is speculation and irresponsible. But no one outside the financial community has so far ever understood or accepted this. Hence the exporters, especially those that export from countries with a strong currency, that is, one with positive balances of trade and payments, find themselves between the devil and the deep blue sea. If they do not hedge, they endanger their company and with it the jobs of their employes. If they do, they risk being branded as "speculators" and will be blamed for the very currency disorders they are trying to escape. Once all currencies have become political counters, large exporters have no alternative but to demand some form of transnational money for their liquid funds, their receivables, their monetary balances. Their need becomes even more acute as more and more of the countries with strong currencies— Switzerland for instance, or even West Germany—are being forced by the instability of the weak or manipulated currencies to protect themselves against imported inflation by closing their borders to "flight capital" from abroad.

The other main group of holders of liquid funds in the world economy, the OPEC countries and especially the OPEC countries with relatively small populations, cannot invest in their own countries; there is little to invest in. They must keep their funds outside their own countries, and this means in foreign currencies.

To the outside petroleum-importing world, OPEC appears a huge success. But from inside OPEC, the cartel must seem a gigantic failure and the years since 1973 a period of bitter frustration and disappointment. In terms of purchasing power, the OPEC countries have seen their income shrink steadily from the moment they raised petroleum prices fourfold in the fall of 1973. By 1978, before the upheaval in Iran created a politically induced petroleum shortage and panicky overreaction (especially in the United States), the actual price received by the petroleum-exporting countries for crude oil reverted back again to what it had been before 1973 in terms of purchasing power. The U.S. dollar which is used for petroleum payments had lost roughly half its value. In 1973 one dollar bought 360 yen. In the fall of 1978, the rate was down to 180 or 190. And the depreciation of the dollar against the other strong currencies, such as the German mark or the Swiss franc, was of about the same magnitude or greater. In marks or yen, the OPEC countries thus received only about twice what they had received in 1973. The prices of the goods the petroleum-producing countries buy—primarily capital goods and manufactured goods of substantial technological content—have at least doubled in marks or yen since 1973 and increased fourfold in dollars. In other words, the increase in the price of crude oil was matched, and sometimes overmatched, by the increase in the price of the goods the oil producers bought with the proceeds of their crude oil.

This was bound to happen. No cartel has ever been able to increase its income in real money unless there is an actual shortage of production and in fact of the capacity to produce. But in terms of physical supply, let alone potential supply, there is an abundance of petroleum, at least for the next ten or fifteen years. Such shortages as exist are being caused, in part, by restrictions on output on the part of petroleum-producing countries; in large part by U.S. government policies such as price controls, which encourage wasteful consumption and discourage production; and lastly by political turmoil such as the upheaval in Iran in 1978–79. Under such circumstances, as cartel theory has known for a century, a cartel cannot succeed in increasing the price of its product in real money. It will either be forced to cut back price—which is what would have happened had there been fixed exchange rates between 1973 and 1978—or the increase in the cartel's price will be offset or nullified by equally great increases in the price of the goods the members of the cartel buy with the proceeds from the sale of their own product.

Whether it was well advised for the United States to enable the petroleum cartel to maintain its listed price and to allow, if not encourage, the destruction of the value of the dollar is a political rather than an economic question. But there is no doubt that the American government, beginning with Henry Kissinger, deliberately sacrificed the dollar to maintain the petroleum cartel and thus to maintain the uneasy truce in the Mideast. Dr. Kissinger has repeatedly been reported to have said, "Paying more for petroleum is still cheaper than one day of fighting in the Mideast." Maybe this gamble will eventually pay off.

It is not surprising, however, that the petroleum-producing countries do not understand why they could not get the earnings they so confidently expected. They could not have accepted reality even if they understood it. From their point of view, the fruits of their victory were somehow snatched from them by clever currency manipulation. They are therefore pressing to have their income guaranteed against the constant depreciation of the currencies in which they receive it—and especially against the constant depreciation of the traditional currency of world trade, the American dollar. The petroleum-producing countries must increasingly demand that their deposits in the world banking system are held in a form that safeguards the purchasing power of their money. This can be done by making the deposits convertible into a number of currencies, enabling the depositor to take out his deposits in the currency that has suffered the least depreciation. It can also be done by relating the nominal value of the deposit to the commodity price index or the manufacturer's wholesale price index in the industrial countries, thus indexing the deposit against inflation. And it can be done by a gold clause. All three of these ways of protecting deposits in the world banking system against inflation and depreciation are increasingly being resorted to by the main holders of liquid funds, the main exporters and the OPEC countries. Neither has any choice as long as the main countries, and especially the United States, treat their currencies as "domestic affairs" and subordinate their external value to domestic political expediency.

But as soon as even a small part of the deposits in the world banking system is held in a transnational currency not denominated in any one national money, the banks in turn have to denominate their loans in the same transnational units. The banks cannot possibly accept currency risks in their deposits if they cannot shift them to their borrowers. So the pressure will be on the world banking system to develop what, in effect, is a non-national, transnational currency.

At the same time, the pressure on national governments to use the national currency and its external value as a tool of short-term domestic policies will become greater rather than smaller. The link between domestic currencies and the world market currency will become more tenuous and more remote. And we will be moving toward a two-tier currency, in which the world economy is financed and world trade is conducted in a currency that is not an extension of a national currency and of a national monetary and credit system.

It is not only transnational businesses and OPEC countries that have come to the conclusion they cannot continue to

operate in national currencies. One American labor union—
the union of New York State's professional and technical
employes—demanded in the summer of 1979 that all future
labor contracts be written in gold rather than in dollars.

The End of Sovereignty

The modern national state was built on the theorem that
political territory and economic territory must be congruent,
with the unity of the two forged by governmental control of
money—a startling heresy when it was first propounded in
the sixteenth century. The code word for this new politico-
economic unit was the term "sovereignty." Prior to the late
sixteenth century, economic and political systems were quite
separate. Money was basically beyond political control except
insofar as the Prince made a substantial profit by reserving to
himself the right to mint coins. Commerce before the seven-
teenth century was either transnational or purely local. In the
Europe of 1500, before the long inflation of the sixteenth
century destroyed the economic system of the time, long-
distance trade was carried out by trading cities, the sixteenth-
century equivalent of the multinational corporation of today,
and equally controversial, equally criticized, equally reviled.
The domestic economy was organized around a market town,
which was the center of a self-sufficient agrarian economy in
which money, while used to calculate, was only in very
limited circulation. And long-distance trade and local market
town economy were almost completely insulated from each
other, the former with free-market prices, the latter with rigid
price controls.

The modern national state was born with the assertion that
money and credit have to be controlled by the sovereign and
that the economy has to be integrated into the political
system, if only to provide the Prince with the means to recruit

and pay his mercenaries. The modern national state created national markets within which both long-distance commerce and local trade were unified. "Sovereignty" reached its logical climax in Keynes's theories of the late twenties and early thirties which, in effect, proclaimed that a country—or at least a major country such as the Great Britain of his day—could manage its economy irrespective of the world economy, and largely independent of economic fluctuations and business cycles, by managing and manipulating money and credit.

But it was also Keynes who first abandoned Keynesianism and advocated non-governmental transnational money.

During World War II, toward the very end of his life, Keynes ceased to be a "Keynesian." He concluded that no one national currency could be expected to be a "key currency," and that the world needed truly transnational money. He proposed "Bancor" in 1942, at the height of the war. "Bancor" was to be managed by a transnational body of economists who would manipulate it according to statistical information, would maintain Bancor's purchasing power, and would provide a stable medium of exchange for a stable and expanding world economy. This proposal was turned down by the American Keynesians, who dominated the Bretton Woods Conference in 1944 at which the world money and banking system of the postwar world was forged. The American Keynesians—holier than the Pope, as disciples usually are—suspected that Keynes wanted to perpetuate the leadership role of the British pound, and rejected his proposal as disguised "British imperialism." But they also dismissed his argument that it is hubris to make any one currency the "key currency" and that it is impossible either to subordinate the national economy to the world economy—as is needed for a "key currency" to discharge its role—or to subordinate the world economy to any one national economy. They were confident that the dollar had the strength to be both "key currency" and national currency, and that the American economists, and especially the American economists in government service, had the skill, wisdom, independence, and competence to manage the dollar in both roles.

For twenty-five years, the American Keynesians appeared to make good on their promise; but in the 1960s they ceased to deliver. It first became clear during the Kennedy presidency that Keynes had been right and the American Keynesians wrong. By now, there is no doubt at all that no one national currency can hope to be the "key currency" of the world economy; and no doubt either that the world economy cannot allow its money to be subordinated to any one national currency.

The logical conclusion was drawn three years ago by the last surviving economic giant of the 1930s, that most emphatic non-Keynesian, F. A. Hayek. Hayek proposed that money be altogether taken away from governments. Each of the world's major banks should, he argued, be given the right to issue its own money, with the market deciding which bank to trust. Hayek proposed, in other words, that the link between money and political sovereignty be cut completely.

We know today that the "objective non-political expert" of Keynes's proposal does not exist—he is as mythical as the unicorn. Keynes's "economist-kings" would be politically controlled and politically manipulated, and would themselves immediately become politicians. But we also, I think, have to accept that the time is not ripe for Hayek's logical proposal to take money out of the hands of "experts" of any kind and to entrust it to the people who use it, to producers and consumers in a free market.

National money will surely remain, for the time being, political, governmental money. But the money of the world economy will increasingly be a cross between Keynes's "Bancor" and Hayek's free-market bank money. It will increasingly be a currency which the world's major banks administer and which, in turn, is geared through clumsy, inelegant, poorly working—but still working—devices to purchasing power rather than to any one denomination.

The emergence of transnational money may signify a major turning point in political history and political theory. It may signal the end of "sovereignty." It may be the consummation of this century's trend for economics and politics increasingly to move in opposite directions.

The world economy in this century has become interdependent. There is no country today large enough, whether in the Communist or the non-Communist world, to be an autonomous unit of economic activity or of economic policy. In the nineteenth century, countries that today seem quite small, the Great Britain of that day or the Germany that Bismarck created, were more than adequate in size, in economic activity, and in economic potential to be autonomous economic foci, no matter how enmeshed they were in international trade. Today, not even the much larger and much richer United States is big enough to be autonomous. The world economy had rapidly become "transnational" rather than international. The dependence on raw materials from all parts of the globe is only one symptom; the rapid development of production sharing is another.

But perhaps the most visible symbol of the emergence of a truly transnational economy is the quite unexpected emergence of a fairly small number of major banks as true "world-class" banks. The precursors of the modern banks, the financial firms of the Renaissance such as the Medicis in Florence and, one hundred years later, the Fuggers in Augsburg, operated internationally. And when the joint-stock bank, financed by depositors rather than by owners, emerged around the year 1800, with the Bank of New York, Alexander

Hamilton's brainchild, the first to be based on the new principles, it soon went international too. The English and the Scottish commercial banks expanded into the British Empire from 1830 on. The first of the truly "modern" commercial banks, the Deutsche Bank in Berlin, founded in 1870, almost immediately established branches in London and Shanghai and affiliates in southern Europe and South America.

But these banks, right through World War II, were still "national" banks. Their international business was business between their own country and the outside world. The Deutsche Bank was probably the most "international" of the major banks of the period; in 1913, it derived at least one-third of its business and income from "international" transactions. But these were all transactions between Germany and the outside world, an export from Germany, an investment by a German company abroad or by a foreign company in Germany, or an import into Germany. Every international transaction financed by the Deutsche Bank had one leg firmly planted on German soil. Within the last twenty years, more and more of the business of the world's largest banks has become "transnational," in other words, business between two countries neither of which is the headquarters country of the bank. The Tokyo branch of New York's Citibank will deal directly, for instance, with the Saudi Arabian branch of Citibank or with the Duesseldorf branch of Citibank; and neither the client of Citibank Tokyo nor the client of Citibank Duesseldorf is likely to be an American business; nor is the transaction necessarily related to American exports, American imports, or investments in or by America.

To be a "world-class" bank requires a broad home base. It requires the capacity to handle information worldwide, a capacity that is not easily acquired and can be financed and supported only by a worldwide network and a volume of transactions greatly exceeding what any one national economy can produce and support. There are no more than about a dozen banks in the "world-class" category. Another twenty-five to thirty large banks, the "regionals," may be able to participate but could not take leadership. But the fact that those "world-class" banks exist—and a dozen banks competing with one another is a substantial number, more than any one economy except the United States, with its extreme bias against nationwide banks, has ever been willing or able to afford—in itself bespeaks a world economy that is an integrated and autonomous whole rather than the sum of national parts.

The emergence of transnational bank-managed money is a consequence—perhaps an inevitable consequence—of the economic integration of the world economy. Even in a major economic depression, even in a period of revolutionary upheavals, the interdependence of the world economy will persist. The developed countries will depend on raw material imports at least as much as they do now, perhaps more so. The developing countries will depend even more on food imports from developed market-economy countries, which alone have the capital, the technology, and the distributive systems to produce large food surpluses. And the common vision created by modern communications will surely persist.

The Fractured World Polity

While the world economy has truly become a "world economy," the world polity has grown increasingly fractured and fragmented. The last time the mapmaker had to reach for his pencil to enlarge an already existing territory was in 1901, when the Boer Republics were annexed by the British Empire. This was the end of more than a century of political integration into larger political units, a period that began when the Thirteen Colonies in 1789 formed the United States of America. From 1901 on, the geographer has always had to change his maps because territories splintered. The first time was in 1906, when Norway split off from Sweden. Since then it has been fission all along. The Austro-Hungarian and the Turkish empires went first. Then came the British, French, Dutch, and Portuguese colonial empires—but also Bismarck's Germany. Of the old nineteenth-century empires, which in one political unit embraced people of different language and race, only the Russian Empire is still left.

In 1914, at the outbreak of World War I, there were fifty independent countries in the world, twenty of them in Europe and twenty in the Americas. Today, there are almost two hundred, some of them smaller than a county or a township in traditional European countries, and much smaller than counties in the western part of the United States. Still, all claim to be "sovereign," with their own armed services, their own bureaucracy, their own diplomatic corps, their own seat in the United Nations—and their own capacity to make a nuclear bomb.

The age of fission is not over yet. Only a bold man would predict that Canada will still be one country by the end of this century; or Belgium; or Spain, considering the Basque separatism in the north; or even the United Kingdom, considering the pull of Scots nationalism. For that matter, only a bold man would be confident that the Russian Empire—the empire of the czars, of Lenin, of Stalin—will still be around by the year 2000.

Yet so far there is no alternative on the horizon to the national state as the unit of political integration. All attempts to create supernational units have failed. They look much less likely today than when the League of Nations was born, or even when the United Nations was created thirty-five years ago.

There is thus an increasing conflict between the fundamental trends in the economy, which push toward integration, and the fundamental trends in the world polity, which push toward fission. And there is an increasing conflict between the pretensions of the political authority, the government of the national state, and the reality of its impotence in the economic sphere. The period after World War II started with the most arrogant assertion of control of the economy on the part of the national state, the Keynesianism of the 1930s, which, in the forties and fifties, became the received wisdom in practically all developed countries. But the only effective policies in the post-World War II period have been those that accepted the dominance of the world economy. Japan and Germany emerged as the most successful governmental managers of the economy, precisely because they based themselves on the novel premise that national economic policy begins with careful assessment of the world economy. The Japanese, for instance, started their rapid growth in the early fifties with a thorough analysis of industrial and technological trends in the world economy. This led them to direct their domestic economic development away from the traditional industries, such as textiles, which every other developed country tried to protect, and toward high-technology consumer industries like cameras, tape recorders, automobiles, radios, and television sets. The Germans, primarily under the leadership of their big banks, proceeded much the same way. The countries that believed the most strongly in the power of the national government to control and to build an autonomous domestic economy, the two Keynesian countries, Britain and the United States, have done the poorest. Japan and Germany tried to manage supply to fit the demands of the world economy; they succeeded. Britain and the United States tried to manage demand to fit domestic political goals; they failed.

But the more bankrupt the claim to national sovereignty over the national economy became, the more tenaciously have governments clung to it. As a result, the gap between economic reality and political reality, between economic fact and political pretension, has become increasingly wide. The frus-

developed country" can do any one thing it decides to
do—but it cannot yet do many things at the same time. It
produces an adequate number of well-trained people to
supply most of its managerial and technical needs but does not
yet, as a rule, generate the technology it needs. It has a
substantial and fast-growing domestic market but for the jobs
it needs, will still depend heavily on "production sharing,"
that is, on doing the labor-intensive stages in the production
of goods, which are then to be marketed largely in the
developed labor-deficient West and in Japan.

It is commonly believed that growth in the world economy
came to an end with the OPEC cartel of 1973. This is simply
not true. Growth in the developed countries slowed down,
although in Japan and the United States it only slowed down
to a rate that in earlier times would have been considered
rapid indeed. In the almost-developed countries, however,
growth did not slow down at all, even though these are the
countries that are hardest-hit by the petroleum cartel and its
monopolistic pricing practices.

These are the countries that can be expected to become
major factors in the world economy. They are also the
countries that are the most suitable production-sharing
partners for the West and Japan. For they are most accessible
to the educated young people from the developed world. The
young Swede or the young German is unlikely to want to live
long in tropical Africa or in Malaysia. He is at home, however,
in Madrid or Hong Kong or Athens, and can lead there the
kind of life he and his wife have come to expect, with theaters
and decent schools, the opera and a vacation by the seashore
or in the ski resort. The young American, similarly, does not
enjoy living in a tropical island in the Caribbean, in Bolivia, or
in India, however much he may enjoy vacationing in such
places. But he feels at home in Mexico City or in Rio de
Janeiro, and the language is not much of an obstacle. The
young Japanese—at least the young male Japanese—equally

enjoys Mexico City, whereas he may be quite ill at ease in a truly "developing" environment like India or West Africa.

The almost-developed countries are most likely to become integrated into the world economy culturally and in terms of individuals precisely because a foreign manager or technician can there lead the kind of life he looks for. In these countries the young executive, the young engineer, or the young chemist from the developed Western country or Japan has opportunities and rewards that are similar to those he expects at home and in some cases are greater. Above all, he can achieve. In the true "developing" countries—India, Africa, Jamaica—where work and life are a daily frustration, such achievement is extremely difficult.

The almost-developed countries are very risky; adolescence and rapid growth are always turbulent. With the exception only of the Chinese countries and South Korea, they will also have an acute population problem and will be in severe social ferment unless they can find production-sharing jobs for the large masses of young people coming into adulthood. To offset the ravages of the OPEC cartel, they have to go heavily into debt. In most of those countries—again the Chinese countries are the exception—powerful sentiments militate against integration into the world economy and especially against production sharing. Traditional economic nationalism in these countries will surely demand that manufacturing industry be home-owned, be fully integrated, and produce for the domestic market only. But this is the quickest way to stymie economic development in these countries and the exact opposite of what they now need to become major economic powers twenty-five years hence. These countries therefore may be threatened by social and economic turbulence, be prone to the sudden financial panic that is typical of an "almost-developed" country, and suffer severe attacks of xenophobia. They may, in other words, look and sound as brash and behave as bumptiously as the United States at the same stage in its development, in the late nineteenth and early twentieth century. But they may also offer growth opportunities similar to those the United States offered then.

Despite all the rhetoric, the "developing" countries during the post-World War II period were not important (as has been said earlier) to businesses in the developed world. Except for extractive industries and banking, very little developed world investment went into developing countries, probably less than at any period in the nineteenth century. Businesses in developed countries invested in developed countries, produced in developed countries, and marketed in developed countries. In the truly "developing" countries—whether India or Africa—I expect that not much will change in the next twenty years. But the almost-developed countries will become more and more important as partners in production sharing, as the sources of parts, components, and stages of production; as areas of business activity and investment; and indeed, even as areas of marketing as their domestic markets grow. The almost-developed countries promise to change the economic map of the world as much in the next twenty-five years as the development of Japan into an economic "superpower" changed the economic map of the world in the thirty years after World War II.

It is currently fashionable to consider "economic development" to have been a failure. But this is simply one of the idiocies of the day. Never before in history was economic development both as fast and as broadly based as in the thirty years since 1950. It not only reached, it exceeded the extravagant development goals proclaimed thirty years ago, and even the more grandiose development goals of President Kennedy's "Alliance for Progress." This growth took place despite the totally unexpected drop in infant mortality in the developing countries (discussed earlier) that resulted in the explosive growth in population. Although the "population explosion" converted absolute national growth rates into per capita rates of "only" 2 to 3 percent per year, these rates are still faster than anything seen any place in the world before and a good deal faster than European growth rates of the nineteenth century. "Economic development" in the fifties and sixties—even at the per capita rate—can be considered a "failure" only by believers in miracles.

But what did happen—what we should have expected to happen in 1950 but did not—was that growth in these thirty years was as uneven as growth has always been. In fact, it makes little sense any more to speak of "developing countries" or of the "Third World" as if these countries had anything much in common. Many areas did not grow at all. Tropical Africa, for instance, may have less gross national product today in many of its countries than at the end of colonial rule. Yet the almost-developed countries grew faster during the period than any region in the world had ever grown before. They may face serious trouble ahead; but the troubles will be very different from those of the "developing countries" and will result from extremely rapid and extremely uneven growth rather than from failure to grow.

In their totality, the almost-developed countries represent another United States or another western Europe, with a population of some 200 to 250 million people. Their emergence is, at least potentially, as great a change as the emergence of Japan. They are likely to offer exceptional opportunities: as suppliers; as buyers, especially of technological products such as machinery, processes, and entire factories; and as places for investment. They are also likely to become serious competitors. Japan in particular is finding herself seriously threatened in the very goods in which she attained world leadership, and especially in technologically advanced consumer goods.

Within one generation, some of the almost-developed countries should be fully developed, although still poor in many cases—as Japan was still quite poor as late as the middle sixties. By then, also, they should be fully integrated into the world economy both in partnership and in competition with the present "developed" countries. These are the countries to which the business executive in the developed countries now needs to devote attention, the countries he has to study and understand. These are the countries for which a business needs to develop careful goals and clear strategies.

Most of the headlines about the world economy should be treated with the utmost skepticism. It is quite unlikely, for instance, that mainland China will become a major market, a major industrial producer and exporter, in the next twenty-five years—except perhaps of petroleum. It is almost impossible to judge whether mainland China has indeed made any progress in agriculture, in industrial production, or even in population control since the sharp but short-lived recovery in the 1950s from the ravages of the Civil War. The country's rulers themselves must find it difficult to distinguish between facts and the political propaganda that is being fed them by their own subordinates in the Communist Party. China may have to buy food to escape major famine. But apart from that, China will probably be able to buy only if the seller pays for it, for example, through "loans" that are virtually gifts such as those the Japanese have been extending to create employment in Japanese heavy industry. The Soviet bloc also is unlikely to be able to pay for much except food and energy; it is grossly overborrowed today and probably the worst credit risk around.

But one also has to be skeptical of the popular assertion that the balance of economic power is swinging toward the suppliers of materials and, all told, of any prediction of "shortages." The terms of trade are almost certain to shift even more drastically in favor of the developed countries and against the developing raw-material-producing ones than they did during the first seventy-five years of this century.

In the first place, the materials most likely to be in shortest supply are foodstuffs. And the only large food surpluses are in developed market-economy countries: the United States, Canada, western Europe. Brazil has the potential to become a major exporter of food other than coffee, but so far Brazilian agriculture is still that of a pre-industrial country. Japan could greatly increase her food production, especially of animal proteins; but she would still remain a net food importer. The pre-industrial countries have neither the capital nor the trained manpower on the farm nor the distributive system to increase their food production any faster than they increase in population, if that fast. The fact that agricultural productivity since 1900 has gone up so fast in developed, industrial countries—contrary to what everyone in the nineteenth century, including Marx, considered a law of nature—underlies the steady deterioration of the terms of trade of the pre-industrial "developing" countries of this century. The trend can only be reversed if and when pre-industrial countries succeed in industrializing themselves so that farming becomes an industry and ceases to be a way of life.

As to energy, all future sources to replace or complement petroleum are either located in developed countries (coal, for instance, mainly in North America) or require both tremendous capital investment and high technology. Indeed, by the early twenty-first century, the United States should be the world's leading energy exporter.

Finally, there is no shortage whatever of industrial raw materials; all important industrial materials—fibers, metals, and minerals—are in oversupply. Such shortages as will exist will be politically caused. They will be results, in large measure, of the deterioration of the terms of trade of the materials-producing pre-industrial countries and of the tensions this is likely to create. Attempts of the Third World countries to change the terms of trade, through cartels, for example, are unlikely to bear results. Indeed, the position of countries that are truly primary producers—Indian agriculture, for instance—may be worsened by the emergence of the "almost-developed" countries which, as they leave the Third World behind, should themselves become increasingly productive and efficient producers of primary materials.

Adding to the turbulence will be the absence of a realistic and accepted theory for the post-Keynesian world economy. How long government economists in the developed countries, and especially in the United States and Great Britain, will cling to their Keynesian shibboleths is hard to say. They feed the egos of economists and politicians far too well to be easily discarded. But even if we give up the illusions that still dominate national policies in the world economy, there is so far little available by way of tested theory to take its place. And sound policy is unlikely to emerge without a firm basis in sound theory.

It is all the more important, therefore, that the business executive steer by the two fixed stars, the two almost-certain factors in an otherwise turbulent scene: the emergence of the world economy as an integrated system, and with it the emergence of transnational bank money; and the pivotal role of the almost-developed countries, whose success or failure to attain full economic development will largely determine the success or failure of the entire world economy in the next decades.

Business Policies for the World Economy

Business in developed countries will have to learn to live in two worlds at the same time: in the world economy, with its transnational money; and in the national state, in which money is increasingly the servant of short-term political goals. The world economy will provide an increasing economic integration, while the world polity of national states will produce increasing fission and ever smaller units of national sovereignty.

The rise of transnational money in the world economy

makes inflation-adjusted accounting a necessity for the domestic business in any country. Otherwise, businesses simply could not know their economic reality at all. To have to keep different books for the domestic economy in national currencies and for the international economy in transnational money will be hard enough, even without inflation. The large multinationals who, of necessity, keep their books in the currency of every country in which they are established, and who then have to reconcile these books and consolidate them into one overall set of figures, have not found the exercise simple or easy. But if accounts in domestic currencies are not adjusted for inflation, it becomes literally impossible to reconcile the books for different countries and then to reconcile national accounts with worldwide accounts.

Businesses, even fairly small ones, will have to start their strategic thinking and planning with the world economy rather than with their own domestic economy. In the first place, the data available for the world economy are still reasonably reliable, whereas domestic economic data have become ever more distorted and treacherous—whether domestic unemployment figures, price indices, or money-supply figures. Inflation is in part to blame. It makes it difficult, if not impossible, to compare figures for different time periods. But governments also manipulate the figures as they adhere, in their economic policies, to theories that have less and less relationship to reality and less and less predictive value. Economic dynamics lie increasingly in the world economy. Even the business that is primarily domestic will therefore have to start with an analysis of trends, developments, and expectations in the world economy rather than with purely domestic considerations. In today's large national economies—the United States, Germany, Great Britain, or Japan—businesses had to switch during the last hundred years from thinking locally to thinking nationally even if their own market was purely local or regional. In the United States this switch came around World War I, and in Japan even later. The California market was isolated as late as the 1930s; but the Californian business that had not learned to think nationally went under in the Depression, no matter how strong its position in the California market. Now businesses will have to learn to think in terms of the world economy even if their own market and business is—or appears to be—primarily national.

Until the early fifties, international business tended to be organized as a domestic company with an "international division." Within the last thirty years, even medium-sized businesses have learned to organize themselves either by major geographic areas or by worldwide product divisions coordinated within geographic areas such as North America, Europe, and so on. But this recent organization structure will soon prove inadequate. Instead of geographic units, the proper division of organizational components is likely to be by stages of development: one or two major organizational components for business in the developed countries; one for the almost-developed ones (perhaps the most important of the units in which the most critical decisions and the greatest risks will have to be taken); one for the raw materials producers; and one perhaps for the truly backward areas that might be of importance as export markets for specific businesses. It might indeed be desirable to have an additional totally non-geographical unit for the businesses that are integrated across geographic lines through production sharing. The main objection to such a structure—that it imposes too heavy a travelling load on the coordinating executives—will largely be met by the increasing reliance on electronic "meetings" (see Part 2). If we continue to organize by geography rather than by stages of development, we will put areas with quite different managerial and entrepreneurial problems, opportunities, and characteristics into one organizational basket. Structure has to follow strategy; and strategy in the world economy is bound to change—in part under the impact of production sharing, in part because of the rapid change in the position and importance of the almost-developed countries.

Finally, top management structure will have to be adjusted to the new realities. Not so long ago, top management even in the most internationally-minded business acted primarily as the top management of the domestic business. It gave attention to things "outside" or "abroad" whenever it had time. Far too many companies, even large ones, still have a top management which, in effect, manages the domestic company full time and "the rest" part time. These companies then fail to benefit from the tremendous expansion of the world economy. The leading example is General Motors, which outside of North America has done amazingly poorly in the last thirty years, despite overwhelming advantage at the start—the main reason being that GM's top management in Detroit, until very recently, was the top management of GM-USA. No one in Detroit really had time or interest for the world automobile market, or really understood it. Able executives in GM did not go into foreign work if they could help it; it led nowhere. Ford in the same period overtook GM outside of the United States and on the world market largely because it was set up on a global basis, with Ford-North America only one of the geographic divisions, having its own separate management.

From now on, medium-sized businesses and even many fairly small ones will have to organize their top management so that the chief executive manages worldwide rather than any one geographic unit. Otherwise top management will neglect and slight the world economy, will not get to understand it, will be defenseless against its threats, and will fail to avail itself of its opportunities. But also, with production sharing—where relationships of necessity are those of a confederation rather than those of a hierarchy—the top man or top group has to be available to deal with partners worldwide rather than with subordinates. Otherwise his company will have no partners.

The Employe Society

In the social sphere, management in the developed countries faces its greatest opportunity and its greatest danger in the next few years. Society in the developed countries has become an employe society. This offers management the opportunity to establish its legitimacy on a new, strong, and permanent basis. It also threatens management with the loss of both legitimacy and autonomy. The labor union is threatened with loss of function, but the power vacuum left by management gives it one last chance of perpetuating its power even though it no longer can serve its original social purpose.

In every developed country, employes through their wages and salaries receive most—almost all—of the national product. In every developed country, between 85 and 90 percent of the economy's product is being paid out in the form of wages and salaries. And most of the rest is in effect also salary; the compensation of the self-employed, whether professionals (such as physicians) or shopkeepers, is not "profit" and surely not "return on capital," but compensation for labor service rendered. Even the bulk of the reported "earnings" of American business are actually also employe income, that is, deferred wages. They are primarily used to build up employe retirement funds or are being paid to such funds as dividends on the securities they hold; together, these two items account for something like two-thirds of the post-tax earnings of American business. There is very little actually left to cover the costs of capital and to form capital for the future.

The old Marxist definition of the "exploiter" is someone who receives income without working for it and at the expense of the "toiling masses." In developed countries, the only groups whom this definition now fits are the "disadvantaged," the non-working and officially "poor" who are being maintained at the expense of the working people. In the United States—where "transfer payments" may still be somewhat lower than in western Europe—the "disadvantaged" family now receives a larger income out of transfer payments than the average blue-collar working family earns through its labor. Payments under welfare programs and Social Security are not being taxed and the substantial non-cash income paid out in the form of food stamps, rent subsidies, or health care is not counted as "income" in the official figures. As a result, the recipients of transfer payments actually receive the equivalent of $10,000 to $11,000 a year pre-tax per household, which is more than the average blue-collar household earns unless there are two breadwinners. In traditional Marxist terms, the recipients of the transfer payments could thus justly be called "exploiters"; but no one, I imagine, would call them "capitalists."

Insofar as a "capitalist" is the owner of the means of production—again the standard Marxist definition—the only "capitalists" are the country's employes. In one way or another, the economy of every developed country and the businesses within it are run for their benefit. Only in the United States are the employes actually the owners so far, or at least, in legal terms, the "beneficial owners." Through their pension funds, the employes of American business own almost a third of the equity capital of the publicly owned companies, that is, of all large American businesses.* Other employe pension funds—those of the self-employed or those that employes in companies without formal pension plans set up for themselves—own another 5 to 10 percent of America's equity capital; some estimates run even higher. Employes

---

*See *The Unseen Revolution: How Pension Fund Socialism Came to America.*

through their pension funds thus own anywhere between one-third and two-fifths of the equity capital of American industry. These employe pension funds are the only large owners, the only ones that fit the traditional definition of the "capitalist."

Elsewhere the same reality is institutionalized differently. Most instructive is, perhaps, Japan.

"Lifetime employment" means that the Japanese enterprise is run for the benefit of the employes. The right of the employe to his job takes precedence over everything and everybody else. This closely resembles the most orthodox definition of "property"; Japanese tradition waives the right to "lifetime employment" only in the event of bankruptcy or insolvency of the enterprise—the same rule that has always set limits to conventional ownership rights. Equity ownership in Japan is largely a symbol of supplier-customer relationships rather than "property" in the legal sense. Capital itself is essentially not provided through common shares but through bank loans, which are legally considered "debt." But the steel company that supplies the automobile manufacturer with sheet steel will own 8 percent of the automobile company's shares; and the automobile company, in turn, will own 5 percent of the shares of the steel company. Or the automobile company, while not owning a small supplier of parts, will guarantee the bank loans that constitute the supplier's capital. In major Japanese companies, these cross-holdings between customer and supplier run to half of the equity capital—and to more, very often, of the smaller companies' bank debts. Obviously, the holder of such shares is not a bit interested in the dividend; he is concerned with the orders for steel he receives from the automobile company. "Ownership" is in effect a relationship of mutual obligations rather than a right. All the "rights" are with the employes, who are entitled to "lifetime employment."

What the Western tradition defines as "indivisible ownership" is split in Japan at least two, and probably three ways: the employes of the large company in which there is "lifetime employment" hold the lion's share as long as the enterprise is a going concern at all. The banks become owners with preferential rights when the enterprise is in danger of going under. And the nominal shareholders have a traditionally Japanese mutual commitment akin in many ways to the traditional Japanese mutual obligation between members of a clan and devoid in fact, if not in theory, of any connotation of "property" or "ownership."

In the European developed countries the situation is more confused. In Great Britain, the financial intermediaries representing essentially the resources of employes—pension funds, "Friendly Societies," insurance companies—own controlling minorities, and often majorities, of the large companies as in the United States. On the continent of Europe, the controlling interest is exercised through the commercial banks whose resources, of course, represent in large part the community's savings—and again primarily those of employes. But also, in practically all European countries redundancy provisions establish priority claims of employes that approach "lifetime employment." In a landmark case, the High Court of the European Community has gone much further than the Japanese in its interpretation of "lifetime employment." It has ruled that redundancy payments amounting in some cases to full salaries for employes for the rest of their working lives are payable even in bankruptcy if the employer has assets other than those of the company that went bankrupt.

In the employe society only employes are indeed likely to be the "capitalists" or the "owners" of large business. Individually, of course, employes are not rich, as a rule; they are at best affluent. Collectively, however, employes are the only available source for the enormous sums of capital that are needed in the economy. Modern economy has outmoded the "capitalist" by its very progress as a "capitalist" economy. This has made the capital sums needed for investment so large as to render it virtually impossible for any one rich man or group of rich men to supply them.

One of Karl Marx's most acute insights was the distinction between two kinds of "property": personal property, such as the individual home or other personal possessions (a car, a grand piano, or a country house), which do not give control of the means of production; and property giving control over the means of production. Even in Soviet Russia, and even in its most egalitarian phase, personal property has been sanctioned, at least in theory; individual Russians can own their own "dacha," their country cottage, can buy it, sell it, and bequeath it to their children. It is property in the means of production that characterizes the "capitalist" and makes him an "exploiter." In that sense, there is no "capitalist" left in the "capitalist" world except the family farmer or the small entrepreneur who personally owns a small business employing a few people. Large business is everywhere socialized and the employes are the beneficial owners, either, as in the United States, through their pension funds, or, as in Japan, through lifetime employment. And while neither formula is widely in use in western Europe, the employes of European large companies similarly are the beneficial owners through redundancy provisions, above all, which in their net effect come close to Japan's "lifetime employment" and establish that the employe's rights to the job—in effect, a property right—have precedence over all other property rights or property claims.

The lawyers have never followed Marx and would not understand his distinction. This explains why they have not noticed, it seems, that the concepts of "ownership" and "property" first formulated by the Roman jurists almost two thousand years ago and then reformulated in the sixteenth century no longer apply. Marx's "personal property" is still around. But his "ownership in the means of production" is increasingly being replaced by something very different from the traditional concept of "property"—the lawyer's definition as "beneficial ownership" rather begs the question how to define it. The stake in his pension is likely to be the largest single asset of any American employe over forty-five years of age, whether janitor or executive vice president. But it is not his to sell, pawn, borrow against, or bequeath; and the precise value of his asset is not determined until after his death, when his claim has ceased. Individually, it is not "property" although it is surely a "value." But collectively, he and his fellow employes through their pension fund, which is indeed the legal "owner," hold ownership in the means of production; and, increasingly, legislation to protect the pension of the individual is giving him rights in respect to the management of the fund and claims against it that closely resemble the safeguards of the property rights of traditional "owners."

The Employed Middle Class

The employe who in the developed countries has thus become the only genuine "capitalist" around looks very different from Marx's "proletarian" or from the "downtrodden worker" of labor-union rhetoric. He may still be "blue-collar," a manual worker. But he is "middle-class" economically, with the middle-class characteristic of high income security. In the developed countries, the manual worker in manufacturing industry, in mining, in building construction—that is, in the typical employments of the nineteenth-century "proletarian"—can now expect virtually his full income and because of tax exemption often even more for very long periods of unemployment. In the United States, for instance, his income is virtually underwritten for up to two years or more. But more important is that this "proletarian" of yesterday is now middle-class in his education, his knowledge of the world, his expectations. The only people to exhibit the characteristics of the nineteenth-century working class are very recent immigrants into the industrial world, a distinct "minority" and a "problem": the American black, for instance, the "Chicano" recently arrived from the farm in Mexico, the Sicilian in Torino, or the Turkish "guest worker" in Germany. The majority, no matter how bitterly they still oppose the "bourgeoisie" and how demonstratively they stick to the "cloth cap" of the class-conscious English workingman, have acquired through formal schooling or through the mass media a horizon and competence that has completely changed the meaning of the term "class" in developed countries.

Moreover, the center of gravity among employes has shifted decisively away from the blue-collar worker—except perhaps in Great Britain, where school-leaving age and age of entrance into the labor force have gone up much less than in any other developed country. Elsewhere, half of the young males now stay in school beyond secondary school, beyond eighteen or so, and thus become knowledge workers rather than manual workers. In numbers, the traditional manual worker may still be a majority—though in the United States and northern Europe by now a bare majority only. But the center of gravity among "employes" has sharply shifted to the educated, employed middle class, that is, to people who see themselves as "technical" and increasingly as "professional." In turn, the overwhelming majority of people with advanced education—some 90 percent or more—go to work as "employes" and will work their entire working lives as "employes."*

Only yesterday, educated people were not supposed to be employed. They worked for themselves as "professionals." If

---

*The earliest discussion of this fundamental social shift was, I believe, in a book of mine: *The New Society* (New York: Harper & Row, 1949; London: Wm. Heinemann, 1949). Since then, it has been studied in depth, especially by the German sociologist Rolf Dahrendorf, now head of the London School of Economics, and by the French sociologist Michel Crozier.

they were employed at all, it was as teachers or ministers. Though they received a salary, no one was their "boss." Today, it is primarily people with limited education who work for themselves, people who work as repairmen, as craftsmen, as small shopkeepers. Even in those professions in which the independence of the practitioner was a hallmark—medicine, law, or accounting—group practices are increasingly becoming the norm.

Within institutions this has led to the emergence of what I have earlier called the "double-headed monster." But the shift is equally important, maybe more important, for society and social structure. The status, function, power, and responsibility of the educated, employed middle class are going to be central social issues of the next hundred years in the developed countries.

These people see themselves as the successors to yesterday's independent professional; but they are employes. These people are the only "capitalists" around; yet they are employed. These people are not "bosses"; but they are also not "subordinates." They "report" to somebody rather than "take orders." They work for an institution rather than for a person. They constitute a new social class, a new social phenomenon that does not fit our theories and our perceptions, or for that matter, their own self-perceptions. This explains to a large part their ambivalent position. Neo-conservatives, like Irving Kristol, are fond of talking of the "new class," of educated "intellectuals," who are removed from the grubby processes of production and distribution and who, therefore, are likely to be opposed to "capitalism" and all its works. This is only a partial explanation. The reality is subtler and far more complicated. The people who work as middle managers for institutions, whether businesses or non-profit institutions of the "Third Sector," are ambivalent in their relationship to the institutions that employ them. They enjoy their work, they enjoy their position, and they know perfectly well that they would not be able to be as comfortable financially or socially as they are if the institution did not provide the managerial or professional positions for them. But they also feel awkward and have a bad conscience because their values and their ethos are those of the "professional," who operates and works outside of institutions and derives his status in society by being independent and beholden to no one person and to no one institution, but to an impersonal abstraction such as "the law" or "medicine." They strongly feel the need to identify themselves with the institution while, equally strongly, they feel the need to assert their independence from it. This ambivalence explains why they are neither "conservatives" in traditional terms nor "liberals." It explains why they identify themselves with causes that protest against the institutionalized society, causes like the environment, government regulation, and so on, yet at the same time identify themselves with economic development, with material possessions and the good life, and, above all, with individual enrichment.

They are confused because their situation is confused and confusing. They are the only capitalists around, the only "owners"; yet it is ownership without power. They are the only "experts" around, the only possessors of controlling knowledge; yet it is knowledge without responsibility, function without status.

"Power Follows Property"

Almost three hundred years ago, in 1700, one of the founding fathers of modern political thought, the Englishman James Harrington, explained in his *Oceana* that the "Glorious Revolution" of 1688 in England was inevitable because economic power, which had moved into the hands of the landed gentry, was no longer in alignment with political power, which had remained in the hands of the King and of great nobles. "Power," Harrington said, paraphrasing Aristotle, "follows property." Political power has to be in alignment with economic power, and vice versa.

And Responsibility Follows Knowledge

An equally ancient axiom also going back at least to Aristotle adds that "Responsibility follows knowledge." Knowledge not only has high responsibility. Knowledge has to be endowed with responsibility or else it becomes irresponsible and arrogant. It becomes the "new class" of Irving Kristol—arrogant yet embittered, greedy yet "alienated."

In today's developed countries, both rules are violated. The employes have the property; they are the "capitalists." Yet they do not know this, nor are they integrated into the exercise of power and charged with the responsibility of ownership. Employes have the knowledge. Even the "high school dropout" tending a machine has more years of formal schooling and an infinitely wider horizon than the machine tender of seventy years ago. The grandson of that machine tender probably went to college for four years after high school and is just now attending evening classes to get his master's degree in business administration or his doctor's degree in geology. But in his place of employment he is not forced to take responsibility commensurate with his knowledge. He is paid, paid well, in fact much too well for the amount of responsibility demanded of him. He is held responsible neither for his ownership power nor for his knowledge power. And that, at bottom, explains his unease, his discontent, his psychological hollowness. Today's employe has income and income security. He has power in political society but lacks power in his own institution. He has function but lacks status. He lacks responsibility.

And since "Power follows property," managers cannot and will not be able to maintain their control unless they build "property," that is, the employe, into the power structure and control of enterprise. One fundamental challenge to management in the employe society is to convert the employe's ownership of the means of production into the solid ground of management legitimacy. The other fundamental challenge is to convert the employe's knowledge into responsibility within the enterprise and on the job.

Around 1920, social power in the economy began to drift away from the traditional capitalists, the "owners" of the nineteenth century, into the hands of professional managers, who owed their position and power to function and performance. In 1940, one of the earliest writers on management, James Burnham, declared in his book *The Managerial Revolution* that in modern society power would follow function rather than property or the consent of the governed. The book had a tremendous impact. But there were some doubters from the beginning.*

Professional management may be competent, responsible, and performing. But it still faces a severe crisis of legitimacy because it is no longer grounded in yesterday's economic power, that of the capitalist owner, and is not grounded in anything else so far.

Businessmen still believe that they can have an adequate political base in the "small capitalist," with interests identical to big business and with a great deal of local political strength. But this is a vanishing breed. In its place there is now the employe-investor, who owns through his own financial intermediaries, especially through his pension fund. But unless he is integrated—and visibly so—into the decisionmaking power process, he will not support the enterprise and will not support management. He will at best be disinterested and neutral; and that means that the enterprise and its management have no power base at all.

If the employe-owner can be integrated into the power process and mobilized to support the enterprise, management will again have a ground of legitimacy. It will again have a power base. There will again be a constituency for the

---

*I, for one, expressed doubts a year later in my book *The Future of Industrial Man* (New York: John Day, 1941; London: Wm. Heinemann, 1942).

producer interest in society, in the employe for whose benefit business is mainly run in his dual capacity as holder of a job and as "beneficial owner." But this cannot happen automatically. It requires that employes, both as owners of society's capital and as possessors of society's knowledge, be endowed with responsibility.

Management's job is to make human strength productive. The shift to the knowledge worker and the steady upgrading of competence in the working force represent a very large, almost unprecedented increase in the potential of human strength in the developed countries. It is, in fact, what makes them "developed." Yet by and large managements in developed countries have not taken the initiative in converting this potential of strength into the actual of responsibility, of citizenship. Managers have as a rule failed to take the initiative, failed to take advantage of the tremendous opportunity that the shift from the "proletarian" represents, and have thus not made fully productive the resources in their keeping. The employe in most companies, and even more in most public service institutions, is basically "underemployed." His responsibility does not match his capacity, his authority, and his economic position. He is given money instead of the status that only genuine responsibility can confer—and this is a trade-off that never works.

Specifically, the employe on all levels from the lowest to the highest needs to be given genuine responsibility for the affairs of the plant community, including responsibility for designing and administering benefit programs.* He must be held responsible for setting the goals for his own work and for managing himself by objectives and self-control. He must be held responsible for the constant improvement of the entire operation—what the Japanese call "continuous learning." He must share responsibly in thinking through and setting the

---

*A fuller discussion of these topics can be found in the chapter on "The Responsible Worker" in *Management: Tasks, Responsibilities, Practices*.

enterprise's goals and objectives, and in making the enterprise's decisions.

This is not "democracy"; it is citizenship. It is not being "permissive." It is also not "participative management"—which is often only a futile attempt to disguise the reality of employe impotence through psychological manipulation. Actually imposing responsibility on the employes—for plant community affairs; for their own goals and objectives; for continuous improvement in the performance of their own work and job—immeasurably strengthens management in the same way in which "decentralization" in the multidivisional company always strengthens management. It creates a better understanding of management decisions and managerial attitudes throughout the work force. Just as the division general manager who has had to wrestle with a marketing decision in his own decentralized business understands what his top management is up against and what a "business decision" really involves, so the engineer who has had to think through his own objectives and appraise his own performance and contribution against goals he has himself set soon comes to understand what decisionmaking involves and what "performance" really means. He does not cease to be a "professional"; he must not cease to be one. But he acquires an additional dimension of understanding, additional vision, and the sense of responsibility for the survival and performance of the whole that distinguishes the manager from the subordinate and the citizen from the subject.

We also need to institutionalize the economic interest of the employe, and that is going to be more difficult. The specifications are in conflict. The ownership stake of the employe in the economic system—whichever way it is being expressed—is his single most important financial asset. It must be organized in a financially responsible manner and as a true "asset" of the employe. But it also must be organized so as to safeguard important social needs: the capacity of the economy to change rather than become frozen in the past; and the social and personal need for individual mobility and self-control. Finally, the ownership stake of the employes must be organized so that business and public service institutions have clear, effective, responsible governance.

In some ways, the Japanese have short-circuited these concerns by institutionalizing the fact that business is being run for the benefit of the employes, that is, for the employe's job, and by treating traditional ownership and property as secondary and subordinate. Japan faces very serious social problems.* But if the Japanese succeed in building into their system mobility and flexibility through supplementing "lifetime employment" with organized anticipation of, and provision for, the placement of redundant employes, they will have come close to attaining a genuine community in modern enterprise. It will be a community based on the mutual obligations of the traditional Japanese clan rather than on Western concepts of contract. But it might give Japan the stablest social structure in industry of any developed country.

In the West, the solution will have to integrate the economic stake in the economic system with the individual's financial needs, with society's needs for flexibility, and with individual mobility.

There are at present three approaches. The apparently simplest one is direct stock ownership in the company where the employe works. It is again being pushed in the United States through substantial tax advantages under the name of Employe Stock Ownership Plan (ESOP). ESOP does indeed make visible and overt the identity of company interest and employe interest. It does make "owners" out of employes. But wherever it has been tried—and we have been trying it for well over a century—the high hopes of an enthusiastic

---

*On these see my article "Japan: The Problems of Success," in *Foreign Affairs* (April 1978).

beginning have always been dashed in the end. For ESOP violates the specifications so blatantly that it is almost bound to lead to disappointment and to financial losses.

ESOP assumes that all businesses, or at least the great majority, succeed and make profits all the time. But over the time span for which an ESOP has to produce results, that is, over the employe's working life, most businesses go through periods of severe trouble and heavy loss. Indeed, the majority are likely to disappear over a thirty-year period. The employe already has a heavy financial stake in the company through his job. It is irresponsible financial management to put his savings, which represent his very provision for a future outside the company, to the same financial risk. It is irresponsible financial management to put all savings into any one investment, and even more irresponsible to put them into an investment in which they are frozen and cannot be liquidated. Most ESOP holders thus incur substantial losses over the thirty years during which they have to invest to ensure a future retirement income. Much earlier than this ESOP will have turned them against the enterprise, for much earlier they will have realized that ESOP has been used to finance the "boss" at their expense. As soon as a business runs into even a short period of economic trouble—and the probability of this happening for any business within any given five-year period is about 80 percent—the employes, understandably, become upset, disturbed, and feel that they have been "ripped off"; and they are right. In addition, stock ownership in the employing business ties the employe to the company. It impedes his mobility, and in a period of rapid social, technological, and economic changes this is particularly undesirable. It is in fact antisocial.

One of the major complaints against the pension fund of American companies prior to the Pension Fund Reform Act of 1974 was that the employe's pension tied him to one company. It was a legitimate complaint, and vesting (making the pension claim a property of the employe) was a needed reform. ESOP ties the employe to an employer as tightly as did the retirement plan before vesting. Finally, ESOP abets economic paralysis. It creates a tremendous social interest in maintaining the past. Decaying industries and businesses will predictably be most enthusiastic to finance themselves through employe stock ownership because these businesses have the most difficulty getting capital any other way. But the most fundamental objection to ESOP is that it will create, in the majority of cases, disenchantment, hostility, and financial loss because it violates elementary rules of financial prudence.

At the other extreme is the proposal, now under consideration in the Scandinavian countries, to have one national stock ownership fund financed out of the profits of all businesses in the country and investing in all of them. The country's employes in their totality would be the beneficial owners of the fund's assets and dependent on it for their retirement benefits. If ESOP in the last analysis benefits mainly the business (especially the shaky one) that uses its employes' savings to obtain the finance it otherwise could not easily obtain, the nationwide stock fund will benefit mainly the labor union functionaries who plan to control and to run the fund, and through it the economy of their countries.

In every other respect it is certain to be a monstrous failure. The fund would never be able to sell a share, and never be able to go out of an investment. It would be tied to yesterday's industries and businesses and would deprive tomorrow's businesses and industries of access to capital. The nationwide fund, if enacted, would condemn the Scandinavian countries to steady economic decline. They could not slough off obsolete industries and technologies, but could also not finance and build new, growing industries and technologies. Politically, such a fund, and especially one controlled by labor unions, could not possibly let an industry go down and disappear, let alone finance a new one that might become a competitor to an old one the fund controls. It could not invest outside its country, for obvious political reasons, and could not allow the businesses it dominates to be active outside the country either. And for both the individual employe in a small Scandinavian country, and the country itself, this restriction of the bulk of investment and of business activities to the narrow domestic economy would be surely undesirable and irresponsible at the present time in an integrating world economy. There is a prototype of the institution the Scandinavian labor unions want to create: it is the governmental investment company which Mussolini founded to salvage ailing Italian companies and which by now controls some 30 or 40 percent of large Italian business. Even the stoutest advocates of state ownership in Italy, even the Communist trade union leaders themselves, now admit that this institution is an inoperable cancer.

But the greatest weakness of the Scandinavian plan is that it obscures the fact that the employe has become the owner. All it makes visible is the fact that the labor union functionary enjoys an exceedingly well-paid job and has access to a lot of money. The employes of the companies the Italian government corporation owns and runs do not see themselves as "owners"; on the contrary, the worst labor relations in Italy are in those companies, and they also have the lowest productivity. The same holds true for Israel, where the labor union federation owns two-thirds of the country's businesses.

The third approach is the American one, where individual pension funds are set up and financed by an individual employer (or sometimes by groups of employers in specific industries or professions). These funds are not permitted to put more than a very small fraction of their assets in the securities of the employing company, but invest according to professional investment principles, in diversified and liquid portfolios. This approach satisfies the rules of responsible financial management. It freezes neither the mobility of the economy nor that of the individual employe. But it does not embody the reality of employe ownership of the economy in a visible, effective, institutional reality.

This presents a great challenge to American management. The employes will have to be integrated into the governance of the pension funds, but in such a way as to preserve the integrity of professional financial management. The pension funds that now control the dominant portion of the share capital of the large companies will, in turn, have to be integrated into the governance of the companies they own—probably through the appointment of professional outside directors to the board. Otherwise the labor unions will, one way or another, establish their control over the pension fund by claiming to represent the employe. The claim has already been raised.

The emergence of the "employe society" has destroyed the old base of legitimacy and power on which business rested in the age of the "capitalist." It has also eliminated the constituency business then had in the individual "owner." Then, the owner of a small local business—the owner of the corner cigar store—saw himself as having the same "property" interest as the owners of the large companies. Today, these large company owners have become institutions and representatives of the employes. The small local shop owner no longer sees any identity of interest with them, and in fact does not have very much. He rather senses that, despite all their rhetoric, the professional managers of large businesses do not believe in the "owner-manager," do not really approve of the "family business." But the new owners of big business, the employes, do not even know that "big business" is now "us." Management actually represents the producer interest in society, the interest of the employes. But it does not have the authority, the legitimacy, the constituency, the power base commensurate to its function. And its absurd "profit" rhetoric further obscures reality, and with it management's legitimacy.

The emergence of the employe society has thus created a power vacuum. It has created an incongruity between "power" and "property"—the new "property" needs to be integrated into the power structure. It has created an incongruity between knowledge and power. The new knowledge people need to be integrated into responsibility. Such integration would not take very much effort; nothing that is not being done already by some Western companies, or, in their own way, by the Japanese. But because so far managements have not understood their opportunity, they find themselves in danger of losing their power. The challenge of the British labor unions to the power of both government and management in Great Britain is only the most visible example. There is thus great turbulence. But what most managements fail to see is that it is the turbulence of a great opportunity.

Can the Labor Union Survive?

The emergence of the employe society also creates a new center of turbulence in the labor union. Its very survival is endangered by the fact that our society is an employe society, in which businesses exist primarily for the employes' benefit, and in which the employes are the only "capitalists," the only true "owners." Once 85 percent of national income goes to employes, the labor union has lost its original rationale: that of increasing the share of the national income that goes to the "wage fund." All one labor union can do is increase the share of its members at the expense of other employes. The unions thus become representatives of a special interest that holds up the rest of society through the threat of power, rather than the representatives of a "class," let alone the representatives of an "oppressed majority."

Economic gains, to be sure, are not the only rationale of the labor union, not even of the American "business union." The union derives much of its support from its political role as the opponent of managerial power. This explains why nationalizing an industry always—quite contrary to the Marxist analysis—results in stronger, more militant unions. But to the extent to which employes are becoming managerial and professional, managerial power is a steadily decreasing concern. These employes are part of the same managerial power they oppose. A good example of this ambivalence are the militant unions of university professors. They are primarily interested in maintaining the faculty's managerial power against administrators, legislatures, and taxpayers, rather than in limiting management control per se. This is typical of labor unions of managerial and professional people in general. It holds true, for instance, for the unions of the administrative civil service in Great Britain, whose avowed aim is to obtain for their members full managerial control and to weaken such control by Parliament and ministers. Of course, if unionism is compulsory, every group has to organize itself. We may well thus see a "labor union" for top management people, clamoring with strident voice for the chief executive's rightful "place in the sun." But this is hardly what the traditional labor union was all about.

As a result, the labor union in the developed countries is in profound crisis. Indeed, in countries where they are relatively weak—the United States, France, Japan—the unions may be in better shape than in Great Britain, Sweden, or Germany, where they are very powerful. The American labor union may be healthier for being a comparatively minor factor. In 1980, at least in the private sector, labor unions represented a smaller proportion of workers than they did when the union drive began under the New Deal almost fifty years ago. By 1980, labor union membership in the private sector had declined to 15 or 16 percent of total employment from a high of 30 percent after World War II. It was around 18 percent in

1933. It is only in the public sector, where there is no "capitalist" to oppose, that labor union membership in the United States has grown since World War II. As long as a union is weak, employes throughout society have a genuine interest in keeping it alive as a form of reinsurance. Most employes do not belong and do not have to pay dues. They do not have to submit to union orders. And yet the union is an ever-present threat and prevents management from asserting arbitrary power. But where the union itself has become the power, as in Great Britain, in northern Europe, and to some extent in Italy, the union is coercive. And then it is in danger.

This may sound very strange today, when unions are flexing their muscles and when, as in Great Britain, they seem almost to have usurped the seat of government. But the extreme assertion, indeed over-assertion, of union power is in itself a sign of fear. Labor unions everywhere are conscious of the fact that they have to embed themselves in the power structure, lest they become either tightly controlled by the political power or an arm of government, as they are in totalitarian countries such as the Soviet Union. And so labor unions today are on an offensive that is based on weakness rather than on strength. They know that society still accords them legitimacy. But how much longer will it do so?

When labor unions were confident of their mission, of their social role and their legitimacy, they spurned the idea of sharing in management. They knew that to become partner with the "bosses" and co-responsible with them could only weaken the union. Now, unions in the countries where they seem strongest—Germany, Scandinavia, Great Britain—clamor for "co-determination," for being cemented by law into the management structure.

In part this represents a last desperate and largely futile attempt to preserve the power of yesterday's majority, the blue-collar worker, against the new educated, employed middle class. The British co-determination proposal showed this most nakedly in its demand that the union representing the largest single group of employes be given all the board seats under co-determination. But the Germans also fought—and lost—the same battle when they demanded that professional employes and management people be excluded from board membership under co-determination. The new educated middle class in these countries tends to be fully as unionized as the blue-collar people; and it is often far more militant. Yet it sees itself as a special-interest group rather than as representative of the "oppressed." It may be more "liberal" than traditional blue-collar workers, as the middle-class public service unions in the United States tend to be. But the issues on which they are "liberal" are likely to be far away from working-class concerns: race relations, abortion, international affairs, or the environment. To be dominated by knowledge workers is what the Germans and the British labor leaders feared and tried to abort by their proposals for "co-determination." In that attempt they were unsuccessful and are likely to remain so. But their proposals also exploited the fact that even the blue-collar worker of today has knowledge, information, education far beyond the blue-collar worker of yesterday, though he does not have a responsibility commensurate with his competence. In that respect, co-determination is the response to an incongruity, and to management's failure to exploit it as an opportunity.

Co-determination is not the right answer. The bulk of decisions that affect the employes are decisions within the plant community rather than decisions on the directors' level. Above all, the employe representatives in co-determination are not employes of the company but union functionaries, who have no stake in the company, no interest in it, and often no knowledge of it. Co-determination, everywhere, is a demand of union leaders rather than of the union members, a demand for power rather than for responsibility. It weakens management, enterprise, and the economy altogether, and yet gives neither the enterprise, the employe, nor society what they need. It represents not so much union success as management failure.

Even where they have succeeded in gaining co-determination, the staff professionals in the unions with their degrees in economics, law, and psychology, who hold the real power in all labor movements in developed countries, know what very few managers understand: that the next twenty-five years will decide whether the labor union survives. Management is needed—one way or another, enterprises and institutions have to be managed. Management is an organic function. The question is not whether there are to be managers, but who shall do the managing. Labor unions are derivative and a response to management. But theirs is not a necessary or indispensable function; no totalitarian country has had any difficulty in suppressing unions, as Hitler and Mao did, or in converting them into docile organs of management, as Stalin did. The original function of the union, to get a larger share of the economic product, has atrophied. There is no "more" to be gotten. The social function becomes negligible if management institutionalizes the reality of employe ownership of business and the responsibility of knowledge; in other words, as soon as managers do fairly simple things and things that are their job anyhow. Yet the union today has the power to paralyze society, and the right to engage in organized civil war—for that is what the strike has become. Without this right the unions are convinced they could not survive, and they are probably right. But once the unions cannot obtain "more" for the employes because the employes get "all" to begin with, the rationale for the strike disappears. Then wages will have to be based on productivity rather than on force, and on economic reality rather than on "bargaining power."

No society has ever accorded the power to conduct civil war to a special-interest group, unless it had a superiority in offensive weapons.

Labor unions today are somewhat in the position of the feudal barons around 1300. Three hundred years earlier, peasants had eagerly commended themselves to become the baron's serfs. The baron was then the only defense against the ever-present Norman invaders, who ruthlessly pillaged, destroyed, and enslaved. Three hundred years later, the feudal baron had lost function and contribution. But he still had his armor. He still had his horses. He still had his lands. And he could not effectively be opposed. It took another 150 years before the peasantry learned how vulnerable the heavily armored knight on horseback really was, when the Swiss peasants in the middle of the fifteenth century destroyed the flower of chivalry, the Burgundian knights, by unhorsing them.

The labor union has no horses, no armor, and no lands. It is powerless unless public opinion and government uphold it. This is why Hitler could abolish the German unions, the world's largest, proudest, and apparently most powerful ones, by sending a second lieutenant and ten men to occupy trade union headquarters. No strike has ever been won unless public opinion supports it. No strike has ever been won unless public opinion accepts the union's cause as deserving, if not justified. The unions therefore, quite rightly from their point of view, are desperately trying to gain control of the power structure. The alternative is to become impotent very fast.

This means that labor relations in the next years are bound to be turbulent. It means that unions will not fight rationally, but with the desperation of a cornered animal. They will fight for their existence even if the ostensible cause is a 3 percent increase in wages or a minor change in manning tables. The unions have everything to lose and therefore are willing to make every issue a confrontation. It is futile to talk of "labor statesmanship" in such a situation. The price of labor statesmanship is extinction, and the unions know it. The unions must try to revive and rekindle the old spirit of class solidarity, of virtuous sacrifice, of heroic struggle against overwhelming odds. This, in a society that has become an employe society, means militancy and radicalism, not because union members are militant or radical but precisely because they are not.

Business Enterprise as a Political Institution

The modern state that emerged from the inflations and religious wars of the sixteenth century rested on the premise that there is only one political institution in society, namely, the central government. There are no other legitimate institutions. Modern political doctrine asserted that there are no legitimate power centers elsewhere, inside or outside the state. The modern state began by taking away the political functions of existing institutions. Aristocrats became landowners, rich commoners rather than local rulers. Churches became administrative units registering births, marriages, and deaths. Free cities lost their self-governments and became units in the administrative structure. A great English social scientist, Henry Maine, proclaimed in the nineteenth century that the trend of history had been from "status to contract," and that outside of the central government no one had political or social power. The only organized unit in society that was accepted was the family—a social molecule in a field of forces created by the powers that radiated from a central government.

In that respect, there was no difference between conservatives and liberals. They differed only in respect to the institutional structure of central government itself. In this respect, there was also no difference between classical economists and Karl Marx. Both envisaged the same basic structure of society. Marx even shared the delusion of his most liberal contemporaries in believing that central government itself was fast becoming an anachronism and would "wither away." He only wanted central government controlled by different people, by "our gang" rather than "their gang."

The Society of Institutions

Our textbooks still pay lip service to the political and social theory of the "modern state." But in this century the reality has changed drastically . In this century, and especially in the thirty years since the end of World War II, society has become a society of institutions. A hundred and fifty years ago, every single social task was either discharged in and through the family or it was not discharged at all. The care of the sick and the care of the old; the upbringing of children and the distribution of income; even getting a job; all were done by the family if they were done at all. Any one of these tasks the family did poorly. The shift to institutional performance thus meant a very great advance in the level of performance. But it also meant that society became pluralist. Today, every single task is being carried out in and through an institution, organized for perpetuity and dependent on leadership and direction given by managers in a formal structure. In the United States, the business enterprise is usually seen as the prototype of these institutions; but it was only the first to become visible. On the continent of Europe, the civil service or the university were at least as visible. This explains why "management," that is, the study of formal modern organization, focused in the United States on the business enterprise, whereas on the continent of Europe it focused on public administration and, with Max Weber, on "bureaucracy." But the phenomenon is worldwide and the institutionalization is complete in every developed country.

The institutions of modern society were each created for a single specific purpose. Business exists to produce goods and services; it is an economic institution. Hospitals exist to take care of the sick; universities exist to train tomorrow's educated leaders and professionals; and so on. Every one of these institutions, while expected to provide a service of high quality, was also expected to concentrate on one service. It had "public relations." It was, in other words, expected to look upon other social concerns as restraints. But it did its job by producing the contribution for the sake of which it existed, and it justified itself in terms of one specific area of contribution and performance.

With the emergence of the society of institutions, all this has changed. Central government has become the more impotent the bigger it has grown. The special-purpose institutions have progressively become carriers of social purpose, social values, social effectiveness. Therefore they have become politicized. They cannot justify themselves any longer in terms of their own contribution areas alone; all of them have to justify themselves now in terms of the impacts they have on society overall. All of them have outside "constituencies" they have to satisfy, where formerly they had only restraints that created "problems" for them when disregarded. The university still would like to define itself in terms of its own values. But in all developed countries, demands are today being made on higher education that are clearly not the demands of scholarship or of teaching, but are based on different social needs and social values: demands that the university, in the composition of its student body, reflect society and furthermore, in effect, the society deemed to be desirable for tomorrow rather than the society of today. Such expectations underlie the increasing interference with the American or the German university in respect to admissions, to faculty, and even to curriculum. The hospital, which could define its mission as remedying health damage that had already been incurred, is increasingly seen in developed countries as the center of a very different kind of health care, one of social action that enables people to prevent ill health or, as in the case of the outpatient department of the inner city American hospital, in terms of creating a "black culture" or a distinct "health-care climate."

The business enterprise is no exception.

To a large extent, this shift expresses the pluralist character of a society in which no one institution is by itself charged with the responsibility for the welfare of the whole. Each institution pursues its own specific goal. But who then takes care of the common weal? This particular problem, which has been central to pluralism at any time, underlies the new demand "to be socially responsible." In a pluralist society, every institution becomes a political institution and is defined by its "constituencies." A "constituency" is a group that can impede an institution and can veto its decisions. It cannot, as a rule, get an institution to act, but it can stymie and block it. Its support may not be necessary to the institution; but its opposition is a genuine threat to the institution's capacity to perform and to its very survival.

This change from institutions that had fully discharged their responsibility when they had performed their specific function to institutions that have to satisfy minimal expectations of a number of constituencies, not one of them primarily concerned with the specific function of the institution, has come as a tremendous shock to managements of all kinds. Business managers complain that they have to pay attention to demands that have nothing to do with economic contribution and performance—demands not only that they do no damage (as in polluting the environment) but that they promote and actually produce results that are distinctly non-economic, as for instance, an egalitarian society in which all groups have not only equal opportunities but also equality of results, regardless of competence or performance. In the United States, colleges, universities, and increasingly health-care institutions may be under even more extreme constituency pressures, and perhaps even more constrained than business is.

The ideological anti-business attitudes of Europe may actually be far more conducive to business than the claims on business by American populism, which demands that business subordinate economic performance to non-economic performance and non-economic goals. In Europe, it is taken for granted, by and large, that the purpose of a business is economic performance; the struggle is over who should control business rather than over what business should do. The populist demands on business in the United States, while not "anti-business" ideologically, are even less compatible with business performance than the European "Socialist" hostility toward "private enterprise." Socialists accept the performance of business as a goal. The American populist— whether dedicated to the environment, to equality of results, to making the world safe and free from risks, or to the restatement in an industrial guise of the old romantic dream of the self-sufficient yeoman farmers' community—is basically hostile to economic performance altogether. The traditional Left in Europe is hostile to the people now in power; it wants to take over from them. But it accepts what they are doing as being right. The American populist does not. Europeans who flock to the United States and invest here in the belief that America is politically "safe" may therefore be in for a very rude shock indeed.

In a pluralist society, all institutions are of necessity political institutions. All are multi-constituency institutions. All have to perform in such a way that they will not be rejected and opposed by groups in society that can veto or block them. The managers of all institutions will have to learn to think politically in such a pluralist society.

In a single-purpose institution, the basic rule for decisions is to "optimize": to find the most favorable ratio between effort and risk on the one hand and results and opportunities on the other. "Maximization," that famous abstraction of theoretical economists, makes no sense in any institution and is not applied in any. No one in a business knows how to maximize profits or even tries. "Optimization" is the rule in the institution that has one clear goal.

In a political process, however, one does not try to optimize. One tries to "satisfice" (to use the term of formal decision theory).

In 1979, an American management scientist, Herbert Simon of Carnegie Mellon in Pittsburgh, received the first Nobel prize in economics given to a student of management for his theorem, originally propounded in the late 1940s, that managers in most of their decisions neither maximize nor optimize, but "satisfice." They try to find the solution that will produce the minimum acceptable results rather than the optimal, let alone the maximal, results. This is indeed the rule one follows in a political universe.

In a political system there are far too many constituencies to optimize; one must try to determine the one area in which optimization is required. But in all other areas—their number in a political system is always large—one tries to satisfice, that is, to find the solution in which enough of the constituencies can acquiesce. One tries to find a solution that will not create opposition, rather than one that will generate support. Satisficing is what politicians mean when they talk of an "acceptable compromise." Not for nothing is politics known as "the art of the possible" rather than the art of the desirable.

As all institutions become politicized in a pluralist society of organizations, managers will have to learn first to think through the needs and expectations of their constituencies. As long as the business operates in a market system, customer expectations have to be optimized. But most businesses look upon shareholders as a constituency that has to be satisfied. They ask: "What is the minimum return which will enable us to cover the cost of capital and to attract the capital resources we need?" The textbook question: "What is the optimal return on our capital?" is rarely taken seriously. Therefore, businessmen tend to proceed on the assumption that if they can optimize results in the market, they can satisfice the expectations of the capital market. But management will have to learn to extend the same kind of thinking to many more constituencies—employes, for instance, if only because the market for jobs and careers is as much a genuine market as the market for capital. Its expectations have to be satisficed. Then there is also a large and growing number of political constituencies that have to acquiesce if a business is to continue its economic mission and to attain economic performance.

Business managers, understandably, resent this development and consider it a perversion. It would, of course, be much easier and probably in the end socially more productive if the single-purpose institution—whether business, hospital, or university—could concentrate on its own job, flatly rejecting demands to satisfy other social needs as illegitimate and as distractions from its competence, its mission, and its function. At the least, one needs to argue strongly, institutions should not be expected to do things for which they are basically not competent. Precisely because institutions are single-purpose, they are rarely competent to perform well outside narrow limits.

Few things have been less productive than the attempt of the American university in the sixties and early seventies to perform community functions, no matter how badly the decaying inner city in the United States needed help, and no matter how many people there were on university faculties who professed to be experts on community problems. The values of a political community and the values of academia are too far apart for the university to have competence, let alone understanding, of what a city is, what it needs, and how it works. Similarly, it is clear that the attempt of the American hospital to substitute its clinic for the missing private physicians in the black ghetto of the inner city has been an unmitigated disaster. Private practice is something the hospital does not know how to do and is temperamentally unfitted for. It can only do damage by attempting it. The attempts of a great many American corporations to become "socially responsible" and to contribute to the solution of social, and especially urban social problems, has at best not done serious damage. There are few cases on record where it has done much good.

Institutions have to think through their competence. Where a manager knows he is not competent, he has to have the courage to say "No." Nothing is less responsible than good intentions where competence is lacking.

At the same time, it is no longer adequate to say: "We will stick to doing what we know how to do and resist demands to concern ourselves with anything else." This may be the most intelligent attitude, but it can no longer prevail. Today's post-industrial society is a pluralist one which has to demand from its institutions that they take responsibility beyond their own specific mission.

So managers have to distinguish between what they can and cannot do. The rules are simple, their application difficult. No one should ever take on something he is not competent to do; this is irresponsibility. No one is allowed either to take on what is likely to impair performance of the primary function of his institution—the function for the sake of which society has entrusted resources to him. That too is irresponsible. But a manager, whether of a business, a hospital, a university, has to think through the impacts of the decisions he does make, for he is always responsible for his impacts. And then he needs to think through what the constituencies are that can effectively veto and block his decisions, and what their minimum expectations and needs should be.

This is bound to induce a certain schizophrenia. When it comes to the performance of the primary task of an institution—whether economic goods and services in the case of the business, health care in that of the hospital, or scholarship and higher education in that of the university—the rule is to optimize. There, managers have to base their decisions on what is right rather than on what is acceptable. But in dealing with the constituencies outside and beyond this narrow definition of the primary task, managers have to think politically—in terms of the minimum needed to placate and appease and keep quiet constituent groups that otherwise might use their power of veto. Managers cannot be politicians. They cannot confine themselves to "satisficing" decisions. But they also cannot be concerned only with optimization in the central area of performance of their institution. They have to balance both approaches in one continuous decisionmaking process.

The Power of the Small Minority

Such a process is doubly important in a pluralist society in which small, single-minded, often paranoid groups have attained a power out of all proportion to their actual size.

The theory of the modern state presumed that there would be a "majority" and a "minority," and that out of their interplay a national "general will" would emerge. It assumed further that both, majority and minority, would be concerned with the entire spectrum of social and political decisions. Everything else was considered to be "faction," evil and nefarious. The modern political party arose as a means of integrating "factions" into the general good and the general will, and of converting "factions" into "programs." Since Edmund Burke in England first opposed the integrating power of party to the factional extremism of the French Revolution, the concept of the integrating party has been central to modern political theory and modern political practice.

The change back from integrating party to confrontational faction began in the early years of this century. One agent of the change was the labor union, which imposed its own exceedingly single-minded concept on the concept of the "general will" and of the "general good." But the labor union was still largely adopted into the party system. In Europe, it was integrated into the ideological structure of a "Socialist," "Communist," or "labor" party, which holds positions on every issue and which tried, for a long time with conspicuous success, to integrate the peculiar parochial interests of the labor union into a broad ideological consensus. In the United States, the labor union eschewed ideological coloration by and large, but instead narrowed its concerns to limited economic goals, perfectly compatible with a broad consensus on social, political, and cultural issues. Indeed, outside its narrow economic goals, the American labor union has traditionally been an exceedingly conservative force that embraces traditional values—whether family or church, American foreign policy or the American constitutional system.

But new and different forces have arisen to challenge the traditional concept. Perhaps the earliest one was the tiny minority in the United States—amounting to no more than 5 percent of the voting population—which imposed prohibition on the majority by being totally single-minded and oblivious to all but one issue. The prohibitionists of 1920 knew perfectly well that the great majority was at best indifferent to their issue and for the most part opposed. They knew that their cause would be lost as soon as the American soldiers came home from World War I. They had only three or four years in which to impose their obsession on the body politic. But they also realized that the traditional party approach gave very small groups a swing vote, not by voting for, but by voting against. And so a small group, amounting to one out of twenty of the American voting population, imposed prohibition by making it the sole issue that would decide against whom they would vote.

Shortly thereafter Gandhi in India showed that a similar small minority could paralyze the mightiest power by passive resistance and sabotage. To be sure, if the British in the twenties had still believed in their imperial mission and had still been willing to impose their will—if necessary, by force—on a fairly small opposing minority, Gandhi's movement would soon have been squelched. But when the British tried, their attempts to suppress a small minority rapidly became the "Massacre of Amritsar" in which a thoroughly befuddled British general tried to do what till then had been the right thing to do, disperse a mob by force. It was not the reaction in India to Amritsar that made Gandhi successful. It was the reaction in Great Britain.

These two events signified a decisive change in political dynamics. They showed that parties—groups that try to integrate individual interests into a majority coalition—are powerless against small minorities of single-minded "true believers" who assert that one negative issue, and only one negative issue, matters, and that the fate of the world, or at least of society, hinges on one narrow aim, whether it is not to eat meat, not to drink liquor, not to pollute the environment, or not to risk accidents or cancer whatever the price. Where parties, by definition, try to create consensus for action, factions try to block action through confrontation. They are Gandhi's Amritsar mob of a thousand people in a subcontinent with a population of several hundred millions. They exercise their power not by the support they can muster but by the actions they can block. Their power is not that of assent but that of veto.

Increasingly, parties no longer mobilize for action. The power to produce results has shifted to very small groups, which have no positive program at all but only a negative one, only an "enemy." Typically, their slogan is not "civil rights" but "no nukes" (which now refers to nuclear reactors rather than, as it did originally, to nuclear bombs). It is often remarked that in the trade unions of England, "radicals" or "militants" or "leftists" dominate, even though they represent only 2 or 3 percent of the members. This is explained by the lethargy of the great majority of "moderates," who do not show up at meetings, do not vote, and do not greatly care. But in reality, the minority has the power to block because it is dedicated to one single issue and is basically not concerned with the consequences of its action. It is concerned only with nullifying.

Any individual or group that believes in one supreme value, other than a revealed supernatural truth, is by definition paranoid. The rest of us are sane precisely because we know that the world is complex and that there is no one ultimate value, except perhaps one that is not of this world. But whether paranoid or not, modern politics is increasingly moving from the creation of consent to confrontation and adversary proceedings. It is increasingly moving from trying to find the common denominator to identifying the least and most uncommon single cause. It is increasingly moving from trying to compromise to trial by combat. This too, perhaps, is characteristic of a pluralist society. But no earlier society has carried the concept of trial by combat further than it has been carried in the last thirty years in the developed countries.

The small group with its single-minded dedication to one absolute can be called "paranoid" also in a different meaning of the term. It refuses to admit that it could possibly be wrong or could possibly use the wrong means to its end. If the results are not what it expected, that is only additional proof of the powers of evil. It is never taken as an indication that the group might have been wrong, let alone that its efforts were misdirected. No American prohibitionist could ever admit, for instance, that all the Prohibition Amendment did was make drinking fashionable, despite the overwhelming evidence to that effect.

Managing in a Political Environment

The shift from consensus to confrontation and from the search for the common denominator to single-purpose fanaticism means that the traditional ways in which managers operated in the political arena will no longer work. Managers have always been enjoined to understand the needs of the politician and to cooperate with him. The advice has always been: stay close to the politician, whether in Parliament or in the civil service, get to know him and to be known by him, anticipate his needs and work with him. It is still sensible to know the points of view, the values, the priorities, and the problems of other people—and especially of politicians—if only because their points of view, their values, and the pressures on them are so very different from those managers take for granted, whether they manage a business, a hospital, a university, or a government agency. It is still sensible to know that the things that appear obvious to a manager, such as the specific mission of his institution, are remote to the politician if visible to him at all. It is still sensible to know the participants in the political process and to be known by them before one needs something from them. It is still sensible to look upon problems created by the impacts of one's institution and to think through solutions before they become a "scandal" and the plaything of politicians running for reelection or for promotion.

But it is no longer enough. One cannot appease the paranoid; the attempt only confirms his suspicions. One can only take leadership away from him. Today's manager can no longer confine himself to reacting; he has to act. He can no longer wait; he must take the initiative and become an activist.

The Manager as Political Activist

The new manager, whether of a business, hospital, or university, will be effective only if he ceases to see himself—and to be seen—as representing a "special interest." In a political arena overcrowded by "true believers" in "sacred causes," the manager of institutions must establish himself as the representative of the common good, as the spokesman for the "general will." He can no longer depend on the political process to be the integrating force; he himself has to become the integrator. He has to establish himself as the spokesman for the interest of society in producing, in performing, in achieving. And this means that the manager of any institution (but particularly of business) has to think through what the policy should be in the general interest and to provide social cohesion. He has to do this before there is a "problem," before he reacts to somebody else's proposal, before there is an issue. And then he has to become the proponent, the educator, the advocate. The manager, in other words, will have to learn to create the "issues," to identify both the social concern and the solution to it, and to speak for the producer interest in society as a whole rather than for the special interest of "business."

In the United States the Business Round Table, a group composed of chief executives of large companies, has established itself as a policymaker that thinks through economic and social problems and formulates policies *before* they become political controversies. It has tried to be quiet, has eschewed publicity, stayed out of the limelight—and has been quite successful. In the United Kingdom, the British Institute of Management has similarly gone activist. It has taken a stand in asserting management to be the legitimate spokesman for the commonweal and for the economic interests of society. And in Japan, the old-established powerful associations of top management are similarly moving from saying "No" to policy proposals they deem harmful toward developing policies they consider constructive and in the national interest.

To be effective, management has to build up a constituency that will accept it as a representative of the producer interest and as a spokesman for the general will. This presupposes such policies as the anticipation of, and provision for, redundancy discussed in an earlier section. It assumes that management accepts the responsibility for integrating employe ownership into the governance of the corporation, and employe competence into the responsibility of citizenship. It assumes that management stops talking "profit" and accepts its responsibility for earning the costs of society's future, the costs of staying in business. It assumes that management accepts the responsibility also of speaking and acting as representative of the common good rather than continuing to act as representative of one interest, the "business" interest, in which capacity it can only lose.

The failure of American big business managers to fight the impact of inflation on the taxes their employes pay is a good example of how not to behave. The very few people—among them a handful of senior executives—with a family income of more than $100,000 a year are the only group in America whose income tax is indexed against inflation. Their maximum tax is set at 50 percent of their income; an increase of their nominal income due to inflation does not put them into a higher tax bracket. Their subordinates, however, enjoy no such protection. Their taxes jump, even though their income goes up no faster than inflation. The maximum tax is sensible and socially desirable, indeed, necessary. But I doubt whether it will remain defensible if executives continue to keep silent about the gross injustice done their associates, colleagues, and fellow producers. That the unions look the other way is understandable; they are committed to larger government spending and the automatic ratcheting of incomes into higher tax brackets through inflation is the quickest way to increase government revenues faster than inflation. Moreover, it requires no unpopular political action such as increases in the nominal tax rate. But executives have no such excuse. Their silence constitutes inertia, lack of concern, lack of responsibility, and an abdication of leadership.

Unless executives accept the responsibility of taking leadership in the common interest, they will become more and more powerless in the pluralist political environment, and will continue to be the losers in the politics of confrontation.

The demands of the new political environment may sound like "big company stuff." But the politicization of all institutions makes demands for leadership and activism on the management of all businesses, including the medium-sized and even the small ones. In fact, medium-sized and small businesses often have to devote more time to issues that are not directly concerned with economic performance, and often have to give more, and more effective, leadership. Where the big company, whose chief executive may sit at the Business Round Table, deals with national and international issues, the medium-sized or small company may find itself dealing with local or state matters. It might have to work indirectly through a trade association or an industry association rather than directly with the top people in government. But the demands on time, policy, and character remain the same. Equally, the managers of non-profit public service institutions face the same demands and have to take on similar tasks.

Whether a business is very large or quite small, it operates and lives in a society in which the main needs of the community are being discharged through institutions that were originally designed for single-purpose performance only. No matter whether the business—or hospital or university—is large or small, management will have to accept that society looks to its institutions to attain ends unrelated to the institutions' own purposes, such as preferential employment for "minorities" on the university faculty regardless of scholarship and teaching ability. Managers will have to learn to operate in a political environment, in which the dynamics have shifted to small, single-minded confrontational minorities that can veto, and away from majorities that represent a consensus and can act. Managers will find increasingly that in turbulent times they have to be leaders and integrators in a pluralist society, in addition to managing their institutions for performance.

Conclusion:

The Challenge to Management

_____

The Challenge to Management

> Rarely, if ever, has a new basic institution, a new leading group, a new central function, emerged as fast as has management since the turn of the century. Rarely in human history has a new institution proven indispensable so quickly. Even less often has a new institution arrived with so little opposition, so little disturbance, so little controversy.

It is less than ten years since I wrote these lines.* The first two sentences are still valid. Never before has a social leadership group, a new social institution, emerged as rapidly as management, which was virtually unknown in 1900 and is now worldwide and ubiquitous. And rarely, if ever, has it proven indispensable so quickly. But one can no longer claim that management encounters little opposition, causes little disturbance, and creates little controversy. On the contrary, management is now being stridently attacked. It is at the very center of the turbulence. And it has become highly controversial.

There is little cause to worry about management's survival. Unless humanity blows itself up in a worldwide catastrophe, the institutions that the events of the last one hundred years

---

*In the first chapter of *Management: Tasks, Responsibilities, Practices*.

have created will continue: they will become more, rather than less, important. And these institutions cannot function without management. Management is the organ of institutions, the organ that converts a mob into an organization, and human efforts into performance.

But the form which management will take may be quite different tomorrow. The restraints, the controls, the structure, the power, and the rhetoric of management may all change drastically. In many ways the present time, the next ten or twenty years, will be the "adolescent crisis" of management, which will decide what mature management will look like, what its personality will come to represent, and how many of its promises it will be able to convert into solid adult achievements.

The challenges of turbulent times that all institutions face, businesses and public-service institutions alike, affect all levels of management and all groups within management. The first-line supervisors may face the most upsetting challenges, for which they are least prepared. In the knowledge organization, the "supervisor" has to become an "assistant," a "resource," a "teacher." And the new elements in the labor force, whether women working part-time or retired people, require different leadership than the traditional supervisor has been trained to give. The supervisor has adapted least well to the drastic shifts in the educational level and in the expectations of today's labor forces—and he or she will have to learn a great many things to be equal to the tasks of tomorrow.

But "middle management" also faces challenges. The very term "middle management" is becoming meaningless in the context of what I have called the "double-headed monster." With production sharing, people who are now considered "middle management" and "functional executives" will have to learn how to work with people over whom they have no direct line control, to work transnationally, and to create, maintain, and run systems—none of which are traditionally middle management tasks. Indeed, it will become increasingly difficult in the organization of tomorrow to distinguish the "middle manager" from the "senior professional," and both from people who do top management work, albeit perhaps within a narrow sphere of action.

The greatest challenges and the greatest changes ahead surely pertain to top management. It can easily be argued that fundamental changes in social and political control, such as a takeover of governmental power by a totalitarian party or a total takeover of the economy by government, would have very little effect on the first-line manager, the supervisor, or the middle manager. They might have to fill out a great many more forms, but that would be about the extent of it. Yet top management would surely change drastically, and not just the people who occupy top management positions, but its functions, relationships, and responsibilities. And yet even then there would still be a need for top management, certainly if society wanted its institutions to function.

It is top management that faces the challenge of setting directions for the enterprise, of managing the fundamentals. It is top management that will have to restructure itself to meet the challenges of the "sea-change," the changes in population structure and in population dynamics—whether these are the emergence of the transnational confederation or the changes within the work force and its relationship to the enterprise. And it is top management above all that will have to concern itself with the turbulences in the environment, the emergence of the world economy, the emergence of the employe society, and the need for the enterprises in its care to take the lead in respect to political process, political concepts, and social policies.

In all developed countries, top management is already in a process of rapid change. In the United States, top management people in the large businesses, such as DuPont, General

Electric, or the big banks, spend up to four-fifths of their time on outside relations, and especially on relations with all kinds of government agencies and all kinds of "publics." This is increasingly true for small businesses and for non-business public service institutions as well.

A few months ago, the chief executive officer of a large community hospital with more than eight hundred beds wrote to me: "Five years ago, I spent all my time on running the hospital and left our governmental relations to the hospital association, even though I appeared frequently both in Washington and in the state capital to testify. I have since learned that we cannot depend on associations. We have been eminently successful in learning to understand the needs of hospitals and getting the needs of our hospital across to legislators and civil servants, both in Washington and in the state capital. But this requires that I personally and my two senior men spend at least half of our time working on our public and political relations rather than leave that task to our association executives, capable though they are. The time spent in Washington and the state capital has repaid for itself many times—but I wonder how much longer the three of us at the top of this hospital can keep on spending seven days a week, fourteen hours a day working—and otherwise I do not see how we can do both our jobs of running the hospital at a critical time in its history and of developing and maintaining the governmental relations without which we could not survive either."

More than twenty-five years ago, I argued strongly in *The Practice of Management**\ for the development of an independent board of directors with clear duties and a work program of its own. Now this is finally becoming reality. The board of directors will again be a genuine organ of accountability and a functioning part of the governance of institutions.

---

* New York: Harper & Row, 1954.

But this too imposes new and additional burdens on top management.

It would be tempting to respond to these demands by developing a top management patterned after the Japanese model. In the large Japanese business, top management does not "operate"; it "relates." It takes care of the outside relationships—with government, with the bank, with the industry group, and so on. Younger people, the senior department heads who are the "company directors," run the business. Top management makes sure that the people who are in these jobs are qualified; in fact, Japanese top management may spend more time on thinking about management succession than on anything else. And of course it gets involved in the major decisions. But it does not "manage" the business itself.

There are some signs that Western institutions are moving in this direction.

In one of the biggest American banks, a chairman, a president, and two vice chairmen spend most of their time on outside relationships. Chairman and president have alternated in working on the financial crisis of the City of New York; and in the year in which each of them holds this portfolio, he has not much time for anything else. During that year, the other man is a member of the Business Round Table and spends two days a week on national and labor policies. The two vice chairmen handle respectively relations with Washington agencies and relations with foreign governments and international financial institutions. A group of executive vice presidents actually runs the bank. The entire top group spends at least two mornings together every week and also tries to have lunch together as often as possible, despite the individual members' heavy travelling schedules.

But this is not truly adequate. The times ahead will demand more rather than less concern by top management with the actual business, its objective, its priorities, and its strategies.

They will put a high premium on managing the business, and an even greater premium on top management's knowledge of the business and the people in it, of its problems and its opportunities. And production sharing will make further demands on top management, both in personal relationships and in business decisions.

The burden of outside relationships, the demand that top management become activist and leader, also rules out the traditional American approach in which top management spends practically all its time on managing the business and delegates the outside sphere to subordinates. As the letter from the hospital administrator quoted above illustrates, top management can no longer delegate to the trade association. It has to be active in the critical policy and relation areas itself; it has to have time to acquire first-hand knowledge and to give leadership.

This indicates that in future, the workload and above all the preparation for assuming top management jobs will again become major areas of thought, experimentation, and innovation. We began work on top management structure at the time of World War II; ten or fifteen years later, we thought that we had finished and knew the answers. Now we shall again have to start trying to define the questions.

In the years ahead, concern in management will shift once more to the structure, composition, and qualification of top management and of the people in it. "Top management" tomorrow will embrace a larger number of people, especially in larger organizations, than it has done traditionally. We have learned in the last twenty-five or thirty years that even the medium-sized business needs a top management team, and that the one single "chief executive" is not adequate—the job requires too many different kinds of temperament, has too many dimensions, and embraces too much work to be done by a soloist. The proper analogy for the top management job is the small chamber ensemble, the string quartet, in which each player is an equal even though there is always a "leader."

In production sharing, for instance, the head of each production facility is a member of the top management of the total enterprise. A transnational confederation is a "systems" organization in which there is not one but a great many "top managements," and in which almost everybody in charge of a specific piece of the whole has to understand all the decisions about the entire enterprise so that he can function constructively. I am quite sure that we will experiment with other structures and designs as well. One thing we can say with confidence: the test of an organization structure, even in the fairly small or medium-sized business, will be the extent to which it exposes younger people to top management challenges, tests them against top management demands, and prepares them for running businesses and institutions rather than for specific functions and specialties.

Rarely has a new social institution, a new social function, emerged as fast as management in this century. Rarely, if ever, has it become indispensable so fast. But rarely also has a new institution, a new leadership group, faced as demanding, as challenging, as exciting a test as the one that managing in turbulent times now poses to the managements of businesses and non-business public service institutions alike.

Index

233